MW01505065

Signals of Being

Ukrainian Research Institute
Harvard University

Harvard Library of Ukrainian Literature 14

HURI Editorial Board

Emily Channell-Justice
Michael S. Flier
Oleh Kotsyuba, Director of Publications
Serhii Plokhy, Chairman

Cambridge, Massachusetts

Volodymyr Rafeyenko

SIGNALS OF BEING,

or Verbum Caro Factum Est

A Play in Three Acts

Translated by
Mark Andryczyk

50 years ■ 1973–2023

Distributed by Harvard University Press
for the Ukrainian Research Institute
Harvard University

The Harvard Ukrainian Research Institute (HURI) was founded in 1973 thanks to the grassroots efforts of the American-Ukrainian community. The Institute does not receive any subventions from Harvard's Faculty of Arts and Sciences. To this day, HURI relies on small, restricted endowed funds established by its friends and benefactors to support its publications and other programs.

Published by the Harvard Ukrainian Research Institute in 2025

Copyright © 2025 by the President and Fellows of Harvard College
Translation copyright © 2025 by Mark Andryczyk

Translated from the manuscript
Translation edited by Oleh Kotsyuba

All rights reserved
Printed in India on acid-free paper

ISBN 9780674302631 (hardcover), 9780674302662 (paperback), 9780674302655 (epub), 9780674302648 (PDF)

Library of Congress Control Number has been applied for
LC record available at https://lccn.loc.gov

Cover image by Anya Styopina, https://zemla.studio
Book design by Andrii Kravchuk

Publication of this book has been made possible by the generous support of publications in Ukrainian studies at Harvard University by the following benefactors or funds endowed in their name:

Ostap and Ursula Balaban
Jaroslaw and Olha Duzey
Vladimir Jurkowsky
Myroslav and Irene Koltunik
Damian Korduba Family
Peter and Emily Kulyk
Irena Lubchak
Dr. Evhen Omelsky
Eugene and Nila Steckiw
Dr. Omeljan and Iryna Wolynec
Wasyl and Natalia Yerega

UNITED HELP UKRAINE
Helping people. Saving lives

The publication of this book was supported, in part, by United Help Ukraine. The mission of United Help Ukraine (UHU) is to provide the people of Ukraine with critical support that will enable them to survive in the face of adversity, to defend and regain their sovereign territory, and to rebuild and thrive well into the future.

You can support our work of publishing academic books and translations of Ukrainian literature and documents by making a tax-deductible donation in any amount, or by including HURI in your estate planning.

To find out more, please visit https://huri.harvard.edu/give.

CONTENTS

About days gone by
That remained in the heart
As vivid stains
About evoked scenes
Slumbering in chests forever
Forever
Dream
Dream
Gaze into the twilight.

—"The Conductor," Mykhail´ Semenko

The raven himself is hoarse
That croaks the fatal entrance of Duncan
Under my battlements.

—*Macbeth*, William Shakespeare

Verbum caro factum est
Ex Virgine Maria.
In hoc anni circulo
vita datur saeculo
nobis nato parvulo
de Virgine Maria.

—Venantius Fortunatus

CHARACTERS

Characters in Blyzhni Sady

Vasia Tsvit (also Vasyl, Vasylko), a refugee from Donetsk who has lived in Blyzhni Sady for seven years

Mariia Tsvit, Vasia Tsvit's wife

Stepan Hryhorovych, the seventy-two-year-old head of the Blyzhni Sady orchard community

Olena Volodymyrivna, Stepan Hryhorovych's wife

Kolia Khromyi (also Koliusia), a skinny, thirty-year-old man with a mental illness

Baba Karpa, an eighty-year-old refugee from Donetsk, Kolia Khromyi's only relative

Mar'iana, a Kyivan woman who became stranded in Blyzhni Sady after February 24

Seraphyma, a Kyivan woman who, before the war, came to visit her mother, a permanent resident in Blyzhni Sady

Serhii, a former successful businessman, getting up in years, who immensely loves Halia and his dear Ukraine

Inna, a young Kyivan woman with a small dog

Eleonora (also Elia), a young woman of rarefied beauty

Viktor, a stocky, young man
Liubov Pavlivna, a plump, neatly dressed, older Kyivan woman
Hryhorii, a co-op resident
Vladyslava Fedorivna, a woman who lives in a hamlet near the cottage community

Characters in Conversation Windows

Ostap, Mar'iana's brother
Halia, Serhii's lover, a beautiful woman in her thirties
Inna's Mother, an older, corpulent, unhealthy woman
Artem, Eleonora's husband, a serious young man, a businessman
Pavlyk, Liubov Pavlivna's husband, a gray older man with large sad eyes
Kostiantyn, Hryhorii's younger brother, a young student at Kyiv University's Department of Philosophy
Seraphyma's Husband, a loving husband, the fretful father of three children
Seraphyma's Son, Seraphyma's Other Son, seven- and five-year-old boys
Oleksandr, Eleonora's collocutor who traveled with Artem to the occupied territories
Viktor's Father, an older, strong man
Mar'iana's Mother
Mar'iana's Father

Imagined Characters

Danylo Andriiovych, Vasia Tsvit's grandpa, his imagined collocutor

Kazymyr, a crow-man, Vasia Tsvit's imagined collocutor

Ophelia, a character from William Shakespeare's *Hamlet*, imagined by Kolia Khromyi; a young woman wearing yellow and blue

INTRODUCTIO
AD FABULA

Walking onto the stage are DANYLO ANDRIIOVYCH with an automatic rifle on his back, OPHELIA with a mirror, and KAZYMYR with a rag. Danylo Andriiovych clears his throat and looks at Ophelia.

OPHEILA
Well, what are you looking at? Let's get started.

KAZYMYR
(busily rubbing his beak with the rag and looking into the mirror held in front of him by Ophelia)
Not bad... Please, Danylo Andriiovych, it's time to begin.

DANYLO ANDRIIOVYCH
Glory to Ukraine!

OPHELIA AND KAZYMYR
Glory to its heroes!

Danylo Andriiovych removes the rifle off his back and begins to shoot rounds above the heads of the audience. When the cartridge empties, he calmly returns the rifle to his back.

OPHELIA

Dear audience, readers, and everyone involved! These loud but quite symbolic rounds ought to demonstrate the general theme of our artistic statement.

KAZYMYR

It is tied to the war.

DANYLO ANDRIIOVYCH

Launched by Russia against Ukraine.

OPHELIA

Like every war, it has millions of faces, hundreds of thousands of victims, and thousands of true heroes.

KAZYMYR

About which we know almost nothing.

OPHELIA

So we'll tell you about the ones that we know.

DANYLO ANDRIIOVYCH

The acts of this play take place near the Blyzhni Sady cottage cooperative, located in the forest near Kyiv.

OPHELIA

It is located between Bucha and Borodianka.

KAZYMYR

And between the Warsaw and Zhytomyr highways.

DANYLO ANDRIIOVYCH
All of the characters are very much civilians,
notwithstanding the fact that some of them,
in the end, take up arms. The action takes
place during the first month and a half of
the full-fledged war in Ukraine, beginning on
February 24, 2022.

Music begins to sound. Explosions. The buzzing of planes.
From now on, the characters begin to speak much more
emotionally than up to this point.

OPHELIA
Since the morning of February 24, fierce fighting
involving heavy artillery, tanks, and armored
personnel carriers has taken place in the area
between Blyzhni Sady and Kyiv. Blyzhni Sady
has become encircled by Russian troops. The
people who came here in hopes of escaping any
possible war activity found themselves in the
very thick of the occupation.

KAZYMYR
It is impossible to escape from here, the fighting
takes place day and night. During the first week
of the war, the cottage community loses its
electricity, internet, water, and mobile reception.

OPHELIA
The most difficult hardship turns out to be
the lack of mobile reception. On the morning
of March 3, one of the cottage residents who,
regardless of the bombing, needs to walk

his dog, discovers that, depending on the meteorological situation, the intensity of the shooting, and many other factors, it is possible to catch a mobile signal for a few minutes in the middle of the forest, one hundred yards away from the gates to Blyzhni Sady.

DANYLO ANDRIIOVYCH
So, we will tell you about a very small part of Ukraine—about a tiny, provincial, co-op community that spends almost all of its time on this patch of land, one hundred yards by one hundred yards big. And one that is dreadfully afraid of remaining there forever.

KAZYMYR
Nothing too complex. Conversations, conversations, and more conversations. Children and parents, friends, relatives, lovers. The three acts of the play define three periods of life of the co-op residents.

KAZYMYR, DANYLO ANDRIIOVYCH
(*in unison*)
Please listen with an attentive ear, we'll work hard to make any flaws disappear.

OPHELIA
Amen!

The characters exit the stage.

An explosion. The lights fade.

ACT ONE

SCENE ONE

New stage set. On one part of the stage, the main screen is located on which, throughout the play, certain characters who live outside the occupied territory will appear in conversation windows and will converse with our characters. Behind, on the background screen, those particular conversation windows are almost always present. And, at certain moments, there may be a great deal more conversation windows, like during a Zoom conference. But we will only be able to hear the conversations of some of them. These will appear on the main screen at the front of the stage. The living characters in the conversation windows appear with their dwellings in the background. Those that are already dead appear in front of a yellow-blue background.

A frosty morning. A pine forest, a meadow, the sun, old snow here and there. Along the meadow, thirty or so people move in a rather strange rhythm with their smartphones or other cell phones in their hands. Some are raising their cell phones while others are lowering them. They are all attempting to catch a mobile signal.

Off to the side, two or three people are speaking with someone on their phones, but their conversations are mostly inaudible. To the right, on old tree stumps, pines that were toppled by a storm last year, sit MARIIA TSVIT, OLENA VOLODYMYRIVNA, STEPAN HRYHOROVYCH, KOLIA KHROMYI, and VASIA TSVIT.

HRYHORII
I got it!!!!! I've got two bars!

SERAPHYMA
(*tossing her cigarette butt into the snow*)
Which carrier?

HRYHORII
Kyivstar!

MAR'IANA
(*screaming, with tears in her eyes*)
Ostap, Ostap—can you hear me?!

A square on the screen lights up. In its depths, a heavily hungover OSTAP appears. He is sitting in a chair with a bottle of beer in his hands.

MAR'IANA
Can you hear me, brother? Say something!

OSTAP
Stop yelling, Mar'iana! (*He grimaces and moves the phone away from his face a bit.*) Stop yelling! Where have you gone off to, we haven't been

able to find you for four days! I thought you might no longer be among the living.

MAR'IANA
I got stuck at the cottage! I can't get out of here! I'm surrounded by horror and by Russians. And we don't have a mobile connection!

OSTAP
I understand. You can't leave the cottage. (*He nods and brings the bottle to his lips.*) That's what I figured. Meanwhile, yesterday, I buried our mom and dad. They were hit by a rocket on the first day. Do you understand what I'm saying? One of the first rockets to have hit Kyiv.

MAR'IANA
O Lord!

OSTAP
Sorry that I'm telling you this without preparing you for it but, you know what, I just can't...

SERHII
(*a man getting up in his years with a burned-out cigarette in his hand*)
Do you love me? Do you love me, Halia?

HALIA, a beautiful woman in her thirties, appears on the screen.

HALIA

...with something or when? (*The sound drops out and she continues by saying something emotional, placing her hand on her heart, smiling, yelling, and, finally, crying for some reason, but she can't be heard at all.*)

SERHII

What's that? Halia, I can't hear you! Do you love me? Tell me, Halia, do you still love me or not?! For God's sake! I'm asking you Halia, do you love me or not?! Halia, do you hear what I'm saying?! Hello, Halia!

HALIA

I'm leaving Kyiv with my parents. I trust that you'll find us. We are heading to Aunt Elza's place in Ivano-Frankivsk. Do you hear me? To Aunt Elza's place in Frankivsk.

SERHII

What?

HALIA

Leave the cottage and come join us in Frankivsk.

SERHII

Halia, I can't hear you! Halia!

HALIA

I'm glad you're alright! Okay, bye for now, take care my love. (*She disappears.*)

INNA
(a young woman holding a leash at the other end of which is a DOG with sad eyes)

Mom, how are you? Everything is okay here! (She yells.) Mom! I said that we have everything we need here! Listen to what I'm saying! We have everything we need here! Don't listen to your neighbor's lies, everything is fine here! That noise you hear? Yes, but it is very far from here, pay no attention to that, mom, don't worry, I beg you, your blood pressure is high enough already.

INNA'S MOTHER
(an older, corpulent woman sitting on a stool in a Kyiv apartment)

Her brother's family, including their kids, was shot and killed while they were sitting in their own car! You hear? So don't go anywhere! Anywhere! Stay where you are!

INNA

Okay, Mom, okay. Just don't get upset, I beg of you!

ELEONORA
(a young woman of rarefied beauty, speaking in a high nervous voice)

Listen, Artem, I don't understand, why can't you come get me out of here? It's only thirty-five kilometers from our home.

ARTEM appears—a serious young man sitting in a fancy car.

ARTEM

Elia, sweet child, how many times do I have to tell you, I can't. It's physically impossible! All the roads have been closed off!

ELEONORA

I don't understand, what do you mean they're closed off?!

ARTEM

They are literally closed off, sweetheart. I had begged you not to go to that fricking cottage with your girlfriends! To forget about having a bachelorette party! And now what? They're all home and you're still there.

ELEONORA

I don't understand, you hear?! I need you to get me out of here! I can't stay here anymore! Do you hear me? (*She yells.*) I'm telling you, I cannot stay here another day!

ARTEM

Stop yelling!

ELEONORA

I'm not yelling! I'm telling you lovingly—get your fucking ass over here and get me the fuck out of here!

ARTEM
(*hoarsely*)

Stop cursing! Please, I'm begging you!

VIKTOR
(a *stocky, young man, speaking calmly and even
reasonably*)
> Well, who the fuck knows what's in their heads.
> If there's no other way, then I'll go to Kyiv by
> foot. What do I care where they'll kill me, here
> or on the road?! I don't give a fuck, Dad, I really
> don't! Two houses have already been torched in
> the neighboring cottage community. Why should
> I stick around here?

VIKTOR'S FATHER
(an *older, rugged man in front of a yellow and blue
background*)
> Calm down. Trying to get to Kyiv while
> surrounded by such hellish conditions is idiotic.
> Just sit and wait. Don't rush getting to where
> I'm.

VIKTOR
> What is there to wait for? Well, maybe I'll find
> a weapon and then, in a week or two, after it
> has gotten a bit warmer, I'll head for the forest.
> There are places I can put it to good use there.

VIKTOR'S FATHER
> Well, at least there's that. But until the weather
> gets better, stay put.

SERAPHYMA
> Go without me! I'm stuck here and it looks like
> it will be for long! Don't wait! Be a man and
> make a decision! Take care of the kids, Mom

and I'll get by somehow! Yes! That's what
I think you should do! I'm sending you kisses.
Drive the older people and the kids out of
there. Get them out of there, my dear! Love you
too. You too, my dear. Okay. Talk later! (*She
turns off the smartphone, lights up a cigarette,
takes a drag and shouts into the forest.*) You
fucking bastards, damn Russians, you bastards,
bastards, bastards!

LIUBOV PAVLIVNA
(*a plump, neatly dressed older woman, speaking in
a gentle, pleasant voice, smiles at the sun that has
suddenly appeared from behind the clouds*)
Don't forget to water the flowers, Pavlyk, water
the flowers!

PAVLYK *appears—a gray, older man with large sad eyes.*

PAVLYK
I do water them! But still you don't return!
What's going on there? Are you being shot at?

LIUBOV PAVLIVNA
It's so good to hear that you are watering the
flowers! And don't forget to take Barsyk for a
walk! You are in my thoughts every day, every
minute! I'm thinking about you. I love you!

*Pavlyk begins to cry like child, tries to contain his
weeping, but to no avail.*

LIUBOV PAVLIVNA
(*tenderly*)
Oh don't cry, Pavlyk, don't cry. Because then
I'll cry, too. I beg you, don't cry. We love one
another. Been together for forty-five years. We
can't die apart from one another.

HRYHORII
Kostiantyn, now tell me, what's going on in Kyiv?!

*A worried KOSTIANTYN appears, a young student at Kyiv
University's Department of Philosophy.*

KOSTIANTYN
What? What did you say?

HRYHORII
What's going on in Kyiv?! (*He yells.*) Any news in
general?!

KOSTIANTYN
Hryhorii, I can't hear what you're saying.

HRYHORII
Kyiv!!! (*He screams on top of his lungs.*) Is Kyiv
ours, Kostiantyn?! Is Kyiv still ours?!!! Please tell
me, is Kyiv ours?!!

KOSTIANTYN
I can't hear you, Hryhorii. Let me hang up and
call you back.

Kostiantyn disappears.

Hryhorii looks at his smartphone, then at the sky, and it is clear that he is praying. Suddenly, Kostiantyn reappears.

HRYHORII
(*yelling*)
> Is Kyiv still ours, Kostiantyn?!!! Tell me, please, is Kyiv ours?!!

Kostiantyn says something and gesticulates but we cannot hear anything.

HRYHORII
(*yelling*)
> I can't hear anything, Kostiantyn! I can't hear you!

Kostiantyn disappears.

HRYHORII
(*in despair*)
> What the heck is going on?!

LIUBOV PAVLIVNA
(*wraps her arms around Hryhorii's shoulders*)
> Don't yell like that, son. Everything is okay in Kyiv. Both my husband and my son and daughter-in-law told me. My Pavlyk has been in Kyiv all these days, in Obolon, and does not plan on leaving. Kyiv is holding up, son—don't yell in such a frightening way.

ELEONORA
(*turning with a smile to Serhii who is off to the side, smoking a cigarette and looking at the forest*)
> And how is our Halia doing?

SERAPHYMA
(*with angry, crying eyes*)
    Well, probably no worse than your Artem!

MAR'IANA
(*sitting on a fallen tree stump right behind Mariia, whispering, and her whisper, for a moment, silences all other sounds on the stage*)
    Damn you, Russia, you maniacal bitch! May you, Russians, be cursed! May you be cursed for generations! I hate all of you! (*She quietly wails.*) Oh, my dear Mother! Oh, my wonderful Father...

The characters who have been taking part in telephone conversations slowly disperse. On the background screen, there are several dozens of conversation windows. Some people move about at the periphery of the stage, they converse, laugh or cry but we can barely hear their conversations. Mar'iana is left alone.

On the main screen, a new conversation window lights up, and, on it, in front of a blue and yellow background, we see MAR'IANA'S MOTHER and FATHER.

MAR'IANA'S MOTHER
    What a wonderful girl we raised! Right, my love? So gentle, so kind. Don't cry, Mari'ana! It's us, your mom and dad! We're here, we are with you. We love you, you're our pride and joy!

Mar'iana stops crying, wipes her tears, looks around, lights up a cigarette.

MAR'ANA'S FATHER

But it's a shame that she went to Blyzhni Sady at such an inopportune time. (*He's shaking his head.*) And that she hasn't gotten married yet. Perhaps eventually she will?

MAR'IANA'S MOTHER

We'll see. If that is God's will.

MAR'IANA'S FATHER

Can you hear that song, my wife? Or am I just imagining it?

MAR'IANA'S MOTHER

My father liked to sing it. It's about one's youth that will never return, and about a high mountain. And something about a grove.[1]

MAR'IANA
(*singing*)

And in that grove by the shore, boats are tied together, boats. (*She's crying.*) My dear Mommy, Daddy...

MAR'IANA'S FATHER

Do you think that you and I are gone?

MAR'IANA'S MOTHER
(*in deep thought*)

That may be the case, but how, and to where?

MAR'IANA'S FATHER
Gone to where? That's a strange question. To Ukraine, of course. To heavenly Ukraine, to the Ukraine that's in our hearts.

MAR'IANA'S MOTHER
We were killed by a Russian rocket.

MAR'IANA'S FATHER
To be more precise, by Russian culture. It arrived in the morning and fell upon our heads.

MAR'IANA'S MOTHER
(*distressed, after a pause*)
I don't remember much about my life. Only you, Mar'iana. As for Ostap, just barely.

MAR'IANA'S FATHER
Well that means that we are indeed dead because, earlier, you would berate that good-for-nothing every minute. Even now, instead of doing something useful, he's drinking beer in my favorite sofa chair.

MAR'IANA'S MOTHER
So we've died. (*She sighs.*) Really. That's why Mar'iana can't hear us. And we don't feel any pain… But it's a shame about all those that have perished. And those that will perish. And those Ukrainians that Russia will kidnap. And those that it will kill. And those that it already has killed.

MAR'IANA'S FATHER
  Listen, you can hear the song.

The images on the screen disappear.

Mar'iana sighs, rises up, goes to the gate above which, on a blue background, Blyzhni Sady is written in a bright-yellow color.

The music sounds. The words of a song can be heard: "Below the grove a river curls, / like glass its water glistens, / and runs off somewhere, through the green valley."

The artillery rumbles ever more heavily, the buzzing of planes can be heard.

An explosion, the lights fade.

SCENE TWO

*An icy evening. The same stage set. To the right, on old tree
stumps of pines that were toppled last year by a storm,
sit MARIIA TSVIT, OLENA VOLODYMYRIVNA, STEPAN
HRYHOROVYCH, KOLIA KHROMYI, and VASIA TSVIT.*

*Explosions are heard—sometimes closer and sometimes as
if from far away. Everyone sits quietly, looking in different
directions.*

STEPAN HRYHOROVYCH
Can't you hear the music? Coming from the
forest? Can't you hear it?

OLENA VOLODYMYRIVNA
What music, Stepan? What are you talking
about? I do hear explosions but there is no
music. You should have taken it easy with the
*nalyvka*² last night, then you wouldn't hear any
strange things today.

STEPAN HRYHOROVYCH
(*looking at his phone*)
People were able to catch a signal. But I, no
matter how much I walked around, got nothing.
(*He's laughing.*) I'm an old guy and my phone is

old. And, when you think about it, sitting in the woods is not such a bad idea. Because staying at home all the time, with all that banging there for ten days in a row, is impossible.

OLENA VOLODYMYRIVNA
(*sighing*)
At least I was able to hear my son. While he could barely hear me. That's the connection we had. He said three words. That he's okay. That he's working in a warehouse somewhere in a safe area. He's lying, of course. But I thank him for this... Although he doesn't hear me... But it's pounding so hard that the doors of the house open and close on their own. And you hear music.

MARIIA TSVIT
Since morning, Vasia and I haven't been able to catch anything. We left right after breakfast and now it's way past lunch time. But we really needed to... Maybe someone will be willing to drive us out of here? I've no strength left (*she starts crying*), they keep pounding day and night, day and night. Why did they come here on their tanks, those wretched beasts?! What for?! What is it that they want from all of us?! From the Ukrainian-speakers and the Russian-speakers, from the old and the young, what do these animals want from us?! Are we really all just going to die here? (*She's crying.*)

VASIA TSVIT
Please don't, Mariia.

STEPAN HRYHOROVYCH
They simply wish to destroy us. They have no other goal and cannot have another one. They are Russians, after all.

VASIA TSVIT
Mariia, please, there's no need.

MARIIA TSVIT
(*attempting to smile*)
C'mon, Vasia, I'm not saying anything outrageous. We are all in the same situation here. You too, Olena Volodymyrivna, should think about how you're going to get out of here.

OLENA VOLODYMYRIVNA
(*nodding her head*)
We're all together, all equally helpless. Our apartment in Borodianka was bombed by the Russians, so this is the only place that we have left to live. Where are we to go in our old age? Who has any use for us? Nowhere and no one. We'll have to survive here somehow, God grant it.

KOLIA KHROMYI
(*a skinny, 30-year-old guy with a mental illness, laughing quietly and smacking his knees with his palms*)
I saw a girl! She swam in the Horiana river, like a peacock, like a naiad, in blue-blue explosions, in beautiful garments.

OLENA VOLODYMYRIVNA
(*as gently as possible*)
> Kolia, button up your fly. C'mon, naiad, you
> don't want your family jewels to catch a cold.
> An evening frost is approaching. Don't be
> embarrassed, Kolia. Every grown man needs to
> tighten things up every now and then. Have you
> had breakfast yet today? Stepan, have you seen
> Karpa? Is she at home?

STEPAN HRYHOROVYCH
> Yes, I saw her, she's at home and looking after
> Kolia when needed. Right, Koliusia? (*He amicably
> smacks Kolia's shoulder.*) Did Baba Karpa feed
> you today? She said that you're being cranky
> and don't want to eat any bread. You gotta eat
> bread, Kolia. There's a war going on, don't hold
> out for marzipan.

KOLIA KHROMYI
(*gets up off the stump and begins to yell*)
> They're going to kill all of us. I'm scared—like
> an itty-bitty bird. Don't kill us! I beg you! Don't
> kill us... (*He covers his head with his hands and
> mumbles incomprehensively.*)

*Mariia cries into her handkerchief, turning away so that
no one sees it.*

*Vasia, so as not to see Mariia's tears, gets up and begins to
walk, raising his phone up high, trying to catch a signal.*

STEPAN HRYHOROVYCH
Helpless or not, we'll see. But the situation
is difficult. The gas station is closed and will
remain so. A Russian armored personnel carrier
has shot and killed people who came to get
fuel this morning. The guy that was selling the
gas survived but said that he's done with it. So
then. There are battles taking place between
where we are and Kyiv. No one can bring us
anything—I have in mind things of immediate
need. Today, all the stores in town have shut
down. The drug stores are closed. (*He turns to
Mariia.*) Do you have any food at home? Did
you stock up?

KOLIA KHROMYI
Those first feeble poems. That hapless first love.
There were no achievements, only futile attempts.[3]

MARIIA TSVIT
Yes, Stepan Hryhorovych. My husband and
I were preparing for the Great Fast, so we have
cereal grains and oil.

STEPAN HRYHOROVYCH
In our cooperative, we have, at this time, ninety-
nine adults and almost forty children, five
infants. Seven pregnant women. Two people
with diabetes. And Kolia. Right, Kolia?

KOLIA KHROMYI
Ophelia swam underwater in the dark Horiana
river and smiled at me.

MARIIA TSVIT
Sometimes Kolia says something that makes your hair stand on its end. Is he referring to Shakespeare there? Vasia—is it *Hamlet*, with Ophelia? Vasia is a scholar. Vasia knows everything.

VASIA TSVIT
(*still attempting to catch a mobile signal*)
At one time, back in Donetsk, I was. But no longer. Now I'm a mushroom specialist. I can sniff out a Polish mushroom in a forest from half a kilometer away.

STEPAN HRYHOROVYCH
Kolia, too, was a teacher. He taught Ukrainian. In 2014, he turned twenty-two and, in some Donbas village, all of his students adored him. Both in the younger grades and in the older. He was a good guy and a patriot. He would gather some kind of information and pass it on to Kyiv, for which, we later heard, he was tortured. Right, Kolia? Did you pass information along to Kyiv?

KOLIA KHROMYI
In Kyivan Venice lived a young girl, where countless acacias bloomed and twirled. A deluge arrived and waterways swirled, leaving lines and cables unearthed and unfurled.[4]

STEPAN HRYHOROVYCH
And, because of this, he ended up in Izoliatsiia, in that Donetsk torture camp, maybe you've heard about it?[5]

MARIIA TSVIT

Yes, I've heard about it.

STEPAN HRYHOROVYCH

And it is in Izoliatsiia that this happened to him. Baba Karpa gave up her apartment in order to save him. And now, right before the big war, in December, his relatives got him a small home here. With no official address and far from Russia.

OLENA VOLODYMYRIVNA

Well, it didn't really help him much.

KOLIA KHROMYI

Oh, treble woe! Fall ten times treble on that cursed head whose wicked deed thy most ingenious sense deprived thee of.[6]

VASIA TSVIT

There are a lot of people in our cottage community these days that I have never seen before. I walk along the streets and am surprised. We'd lived here for six years, and I almost never saw anyone.

STEPAN HRYHOROVYCH

There are people whom I have seen for the first time (*laughing*), although, in the past fifteen years, I haven't left this place for more than two weeks. People, Vasia, came here to escape the war, bringing their relatives, acquaintances. Who knew that it would be precisely here that hell would come.

KOLIA KHROMYI
(*sternly*)
> Break we our watch up and, by my advice, let us
> impart what we have seen tonight unto young
> Hamlet, for, upon my life, this spirit, dumb to
> us, will speak to him.[7]

OLENA VOLODYMYRIVNA
(*to Vasia*)
> Tomorrow, we'll head out to the villages with
> the guys that have cars in search of some food.
> If we are able to buy anything, we'll sell it in
> our co-op for the same price. Do you have any
> money?

STEPAN HRYHOROVYCH
> People came here before the war—for three days,
> they thought, until everything would pass. But
> this is how it turned out. There are people that
> have five kids to feed but don't have enough
> stocked up for even a week. Yesterday, I walked
> through the yards and made a list to figure out
> who lives here, and I couldn't believe it. Where
> will people get money and food? I can't feed
> everyone. I'm seventy-two already, and my
> health isn't all that great even though I'm the
> head of our cottage administration.

VASIA TSVIT
> If you get vegetables, we'll buy anything that
> you offer us. We've got enough money.

STEPAN HYRYHOROVYCH
Money-money... A lot of people have enough
money here. It's just that there is nothing to buy
with the money. Well, okay...

*Vasia once again tries to catch a signal, he gets one and
presses the keypad.*

VASIA TSVIT
(*yelling into the phone*)
Danylo Andriiovych, hello! I can't talk for
long. Listen! Please! Find us a way to get out
of here! I already told you, there is nothing
that we can do on our own. Keep in mind that
our battery packs will last a maximum of a
week, week and half, if we use the smartphone
for fifteen minutes a day... Hello! Danylo
Andriiovych, hello! Danylo Andriiovych,
can you hear me?! Hello! (*He looks at his
smartphone.*) There's no signal and (*he laughs*),
by the way, there never was one. But we had
a talk. It happens.

He sits down next to his wife, looks up at the sky, sighs.

MARIIA TSVIT
(*getting up*)
I'm freezing, Vasia. This isn't spring. It's heading
back toward freezing temperatures. I'm going to
go make dinner. Come soon. We haven't eaten
since morning.

OLENA VOLODYMYRIVNA
(*getting up*)
> Let's go, too, Kolia. Look, everyone is dispersing.
> Everyone who was able to make a call, did.
> Those who couldn't, didn't need to. Evening
> is arriving.

KOLIA KHROMYI
> I believe that you are the light—and one that is
> not accepted by this darkness? I believe that you
> are the word—one that is not heard by those
> deaf since birth? Perhaps they need a different
> Messiah? For them, perhaps, the Son of God is
> not enough?[8] The Son of God is not enough for
> the Russians! Not enough for them! Nothing will
> ever be enough for them!

OLENA VOLODYMYRIVNA
(*taking Kolia by his shoulder*)
> Let's go, son. Because we have enough. We
> need to go. And you, too, Stepan, don't sit here
> for long!

*The women go. Kolia waves his arms, talks about
something, dances, laughs. Heavy artillery sounds.
Someone in the forest begins to sing "There is a High
Mountain."*

STEPAN HRYHORYVYCH
(*listening in*)
> So they're singing that song again, and she tells
> me to drink less nalyvka. What does this have to
> do with nalyvka? It's a great song, I tell you...

VASIA TSVIT
(*smiling*)
   My grandmother loved it. Sometimes she would
   drink a shot, close her eyes and begin singing.
   What a funny grandma she was, a Ukrainian-
   speaking one. That was rare in Donetsk.

(*They remain silent.*)

STEPAN HRYHOROVYCH
   In a village just past Pylypovychi, last night,
   Russian soldiers executed a family that included
   several kids. Twelve people in all.

VASIA TSVIT
(*horrified*)
   For what?!

STEPAN HRYHOROVYCH
   They refused to feed those degenerates. Because
   they didn't have much food. There were seven
   kids and three old people in that family. They
   were all murdered. The adults, the children, the
   old people. And they burned down their home.
   Nobody survived.

VASIA TSVIT
   How horrible. They are not human.

STEPAN HRYHOROVYCH
   They, Vasia, are Russians. That's all you need
   to know. So what are we supposed to do about

that, how do we survive? It would be good to get out of here. But one little question remains...

VASIA TSVIT
How and where to?

STEPAN HRYHOROVYCH
Yes, Vasia, how and where to.

The explosions get increasingly louder. It quickly becomes dark. MAR'IANA approaches from the gates of the cottage village and sits down with the men. Stepan Hryhorovych looks at her with pity and, after pausing for a second, delicately pulls her toward him. Mar'iana appreciatively snuggles up to the old man. Her deceased parents once again appear on the main screen. They sit embracing one another.

A high female voice sings: "On shore's edge in the calm, boats tied together, there, three willows have bent over, looking worried."[9]

An explosion. The lights fade.

SCENE THREE

The bedroom in the Tsvit home. The ticking of the clock can be heard. The noise made by the furnace can be heard. From recurring explosions, the dishware in the cabinet occasionally rings. We can't see the whole room across the stage because the windows are covered with a thick black cloth. By one of the windows, a tall, skinny gray old man is sitting on a stool and reading something, but he can barely be seen. We only notice him when he begins to speak.

VASIA is sitting on a bed dressed in night clothes, half covered by a comforter, and holding a big flashlight. This is the only light on the stage at the beginning of the scene.

VASIA TSVIT
(*looking into the audience*)
> Archangel Michael, Archangel Gabriel, and you, Raphael, Uriel, and Sealtiel, you see everything, too!

Images of the archangels appear on the screen.

VASIA TSVIT
> Jehudiel, and Barachiel, you are always with us. Pray for us! We're so scared.

Holy Mother of God, if my Mariia and I are fated to die in Blyzhni Sady, only thirty kilometers from Kyiv, surrounded by the Russians, without light, water, electricity and a mobile signal, if that is the will of God, then so be it. But I beg You, please pray to Your Son for our quick and honorable death. Honorable, Mother of God, and quick! I don't ask for anything, Mother of God. Just please grant us—my wife and me—a simple and honorable death! A quick one, Mother of God, and honorable! Let us remain human to the very end!

MARIIA *enters the room with her own flashlight and a towel wrapped around her head.*

MARIIA TSVIT
Who are you speaking to, Vasia?

VASIA TSVIT
(*crosses himself, places his flashlight between his pillow and his wife's, and slides under a thick comforter*)
You haven't been around for a while. I was going to head out and look for you.

MARIIA TSVIT
(*turning on her flashlight*)
There's no light, Vasia. There's no water. It takes time to go with this pitcher, get hot water from the saucepan, and then add cold water from the bottle. And I also need to find some soap and do all that without falling down.

*A few incredibly loud explosions can be heard, the
invisible dishware rings melodically in the cabinet.*

VASIA TSVIT
Maybe it's somewhere along the highway to
Zhytomyr.

MARIIA TSVIT
(*quickly, before she gets cold, puts on her special night
clothes, gets under the comforters, three or four of
them stacked on one another*)
It's still so cold... Have you figured out what
we're going to talk about?

VASIA TSVIT
(*seriously*)
Well, what time is it?

MARIIA TSVIT
(*looking at her wristwatch*)
It's only seven, beginning of eight. So we need to
converse for a whole three more hours.

VASIA TSVIT
You see—my watch came in handy!

MARIIA TSVIT
Yes, you gave it to me as an anniversary present.
It's a good thing that it's a mechanical one.
We're only able to turn our smartphones on once
or twice a day now, and it's hard not knowing
what time it is. I'm not even sure why.

VASIA TSVIT
Time's been a problem, in general. It would be even worse without a watch.

The furnace, which had been working well until now, starts to die down. Vasia tenses up, but a second later the furnace switches to a different cycle. Vasia nervously smiles and sighs.

MARIIA TSVIT
What's up?

VASIA TSVIT
I keep listening in to see if the furnace is working or not. God forbid it should break down. You won't be able to find a repairman. It's below freezing outside.

MARIIA TSVIT
You have to ignore it. Tell me something interesting. According to the plan, we have a few more hours of conversations scheduled ahead of us.

VASIA TSVIT
Yes. We can't fall asleep earlier than ten. Because waking up at three a.m. and lying in the dark is even worse. You slept this past night while I, the idiot that I'm, was listening at three a.m. to the planes flying above us and to the artillery that was pounding somewhere near Irpin.

MARIIA TSVIT
(*bundles herself in the comforter so that only her nose and eyes are visible*)
　　Did you often fall in love when you were a kid?

VASIA TSVIT
　　All the time!

MARIIA TSVIT
　　Even in kindergarten?

VASIA TSVIT
　　In kindergarten, I loved without pause. It was then that I managed to fall in love with several girls simultaneously... Did you ever fall in love with several boys at once?

MARIIA TSVIT
　　Yes, (*smiling*) in kindergarten, too. It was very embarrassing, but what could you do?

VASIA TSVIT
　　Did they know about this?

MARIIA TSVIT
(*laughing*)
　　Of course not. You can't imagine how quiet and shy I was. I wouldn't say a word. I just looked on from afar. That's the kind of love it was.

VASIA TSVIT
　　I was constantly in love with two or three simultaneously. It's really convenient, you know.

If your favorite one got sick and didn't come
to kindergarten, or to school, you, through the
strength of your will, activated the next one. And,
this way, you're never left without genuine feelings.

MARIIA TSVIT
Everything was genuine with me. I loved but
didn't play games.

VASIA TSVIT
Me too, genuinely.

MARIIA TSVIT
No, you always were a playboy.

VASIA TSVIT
Hey, c'mon. I was always faithful to my three
girls. Moreover, I dedicated poems to them. (*He
laughs.*) With my poetic efforts, I offered these
girls immortality. I gave them immortal life with
my lines, you understand?

MARIIA TSVIT
(*with tears in her eyes, suddenly in a very high tone*)
I don't want to die this way, Vasia. I want to
live, to live, to live, Vasia. I want to visit the
Chapel of the Ascension in Jerusalem! To go
to the grave of the Mother of God! To walk
around the old city. Do you remember that
beautiful bazaar there?! That pomegranate
juice? How tasty the pastries were by the Jaffa
Gate? Oh God, I so want to live! (*She sticks her
face in the pillow and cries.*)

VASIA TSVIT
(*sits up on the bed*)
   Don't cry, don't be afraid! Don't fear anything,
   sunshine! I've been praying to the Mother of God
   for a week already, asking for a simple death. Do
   you understand? Not a difficult one, long one, or
   shameful one...

MARIIA TSVIT
(*also sits up on the bed, yells*)
   I don't want to die! Neither a simple nor quick
   death, I don't want to die any way! I want to live,
   Vasia! Don't pray for me! Don't pray for death!
   I want to live, to live! You never prayed for the
   right things! Didn't ask for the right things!

VASIA TSVIT
(*after a pause*)
   Well, I want to go to Nazareth. To the Catholic
   Church of the Annunciation. Do you remember
   those images of the Mother of God there from
   all the world's countries?

MARIIA TSVIT
   There, by the entrance, is an unusually touching
   Mother of God. Unusual and touching.

VASIA TSVIT
   And what's that beach in Netanya?

MARIIA TSVIT
   Sironit. You could spend three lifetimes in a row
   there, and it still wouldn't be enough.

VASIA TSVIT
> And how about the Ralli museum in Caesarea?
> The Roman racetrack, the foundation of Pontius
> Pilate's palace, which is always flooded with
> water from the Mediterranean Sea?

Mariia hugs Vasia and places her head on his shoulder.

MARIIA TSVIT
(smiling)
> Yes, yes. So many good, nice things in the world,
> genuine things. It would be great to return to all
> of them... Listen, who is this Danylo Andriiovych
> whom you called today while we were in the
> forest?

*The song "Hey, I Had a Horse" can be heard, sometimes
getting louder, sometimes quieter, for the duration of the
action. The old man that sat at the beginning of the scene
with a Bible in his hands gets up off the stool. He holds
the book under his armpit. He goes right up to the bed,
bends over and looks into Mariia's face, demonstratively
moving his hand in front of her eyes and shakes his head.
She doesn't react at all to his presence.*

DANYLO ANDRIIOVYCH
> I told you, Vasia. Don't call me. Especially
> in front of your wife. Don't do it. I thought
> you were a smart guy, that you understood
> everything, like a real scholar and someone from
> Donbas. But you're just a punk, just a pea-brain.
> One who, on top of that, reads the Gospels.

VASIA TSVIT
(*irritated*)
> Well, then how I'm supposed to get in touch
> with you? How? You show up whenever you
> want. And what are we to do? We need to get
> out of here. But we don't have a chance because
> nobody needs us, nobody! Neither my wife and
> me, nor this whole fucking co-op.

MARIIA TSVIT
(*withdrawing, looking at Vasia with horror*)
> Who are you talking to?!

VASIA TSVIT
(*pointing to his interlocutor*)
> To him.

DANYLO ANDRIIOVYCH
> C'mon dummy. She can't see me. You really don't
> get that?

MARIIA TSVIT
(*frightened*)
> Who's "him"?

VASIA TSVIT
(*raising his shoulders, remaining silent*)
> I've been seeing Danylo, my grandfather, my
> dad's father, for a week now. Occasionally, we
> converse. He's here right now.

MARIIA TSVIT
> Dear God! Don't frighten me!

VASIA TSVIT

I know, I know, Mariia. You never liked each
other. And you only saw him a few times. But
listen, he was a good person. He loved both me
and my parents. Although he drank a lot. A ton.
But that's a different story. What's important
is that he is the only one that responded, you
understand? Especially since there's no connection
with anyone. But with Danylo Andriiovych it
worked out. Understand? There's no internet, no
water, our cell phones will stop working soon!
How will we be able to talk with anyone then?
How will we be able to ask for help? While the
Russians just keep pounding and pounding Kyiv!
Pounding and pounding us! They are killing and
killing us! Killing and killing! (*He cries.*)

MARIIA TSVIT

You've lost your mind, Vasia! My dear Vasia! How
awful. My poor thing. (*She embraces Vasia.*) How
is this possible? You're strong, a good guy. You
should be able to endure. There can be no Danylo
Andriiovych. Because he died ten years before the
big war. Why can't you comprehend that?

*Mariia kisses and caresses Vasia's head, shoulders, hands.
He bows his head but speaks rather sternly.*

VASIA TSVIT

Sure, perhaps I've gone crazy, Mariia. But what's
the difference if we don't have any other hope
anyway. And Danylo Andriiovych will help us!
(*He raises his head.*) He will definitely help us.

Right, Danylo Andriiovych?! Say something!
You're not just a dream.

DANYLO ANDRIIOVYCH
The day's black sun sets—and the heart wanders
stiffly, by the headboard a ghost hovers—is this
a dream, an appearance, or delusion?[10]

*He places the Bible on the bed and disappears into the
room's darkness.*

MARIIA TSVIT
(*with horror*)
Oh God, Vasia! I beg you, pull yourself together!
You can't leave me alone in this situation! You
can't leave me behind! You're a man! You're not like
Kolia! Kolia could lose his mind. Kolia's body was
slashed and burned, and he was left alone with
the executioners! But you have me! You, Vasia,
can't do this! You can't lose your mind at this time!
You need to understand that your grandfather
is not here. But I am! You have me! And I need
your help. You need to pull yourself together and
get us out of here! Get us out of here, Vasia, and
then do whatever you want! Do you understand?!
Talk to grandpas if you choose, to grandmas! To
Shakespeare, or Taras Hryhorovych Shevchenko!

VASIA TSVIT
(*takes the Bible that the ghost left on the blanket at
the foot of the bed, opens it, and reads out loud*)
...where your treasure is, where your heart will
be. The eye is the lamp of the body. If your

eyes are good, your whole body will be full
of light. But if your eyes are unhealthy, your
whole body will be full of darkness. If then
the light within you is darkness, how great is
that darkness! (*He closes the Bible, bends down
and kisses his wife's forehead.*) Yes, you are
correct, Mariia. He is not there, while we are.
And, although the eye is the lamp of the body,
I'm very tired, I'm sorry. I'm just tired and
that is why I see all kinds of things. We need
to lie down and go to sleep no matter what.
(*He forces himself to laugh.*) We'll consider
this dizziness that I have to be the result of
Russian culture that came to Kyiv's walls and
surrounded us from all sides. At this time, right
on the Warsaw highway, are all those endless
Pushkins, Dostoyevskys, and Tolstoys. That
entire fucking ballet, all of that refined Buryat
spirituality. Came to us on tanks. Accursed
hoard. Oh, how sick I am of seeing all those
mugs in the forest! These entire eight years
that we've been refugees and homeless. All
these years, how they drained me because they
kept appearing to me. They would continually
appear behind every tree, behind every hill,
in every lived day. Now, tell me the truth!
We knew, my dear wife, both of us always
knew that it would be like this. That they'd
come after us wearing tutus, with volumes
containing the works of Soviet classic writers,
during the dance of Peter Ilyich Tchaikovsky's
little swans, during the ringing of the church
bells and the rocket hits. That they wouldn't

stop with our Donetsk. Oh, how tired I am, my dear wife! Of the past and the future, of the future and the past. A Ukrainian who hadn't learned the Ukrainian language until he was almost fifty. Why have you treated me in this way, oh fate of mine? Oh this exhaustion, it pains me, like a play pains a theater... (*He sighs.*) I'm exhausted, so exhausted... (*He rests his head of his wife's chest.*)

MARIIA TSVIT

Yes, dear, yes. (*She kisses her husband and helps him to snuggle up next to her in the frigid bed.*) You're just tired. We need to turn off our flashlights and go to sleep. You'll rest. You'll pull yourself together. And tomorrow, you'll think of something. We'll be able to cross this abyss, the two of us are strong, we're good people. And those pastries with dates by the Jaffa Gate are so tasty. Right?

VASIA TSVIT

Yes, dear, the pastries by the Jaffa Gate. The Church of the Annunciation. Golgotha. The darkness that came onto earth when the Savior descended into Hell. (*He covers himself with the comforter, closes his eyes, sighs deeply.*)

Mariia turns off the flashlights, snuggles in more comfortably. The artillery pounds frantically. The home shakes, the dishware in the china cabinet rings.

DANYLO ANDRIIOVYCH
(*appears on the screen*)
　　Roar storm all through the world, mad thunder
　　high above, though that path may not be
　　hallowed—that unforgiving path is ours.[11]

MARIIA TSVIT
(*in a dream*)
　　Amen.

ACT TWO

SCENE ONE

A frosty morning.

An explosion and the lights fade. A pine forest, a meadow, the sun. In the past weeks, once again much snow has fallen. In the meadow, about thirty people with smartphones and cell phones in their hands are trying to catch a mobile signal, they converse, but it is almost impossible to hear what they are saying. On the background screen, fifteen to twenty conversation windows are on. There are all kinds of characters in them: the Ukrainian military, adults and children, women and men of various ages.

To the right, on tree stumps that have been toppled by a storm, sit MARIIA TSVIT, OLENA VOLODYMYRIVNA, STEPAN HRYHOROVYCH, KOLIA KHROMYI, VASIA TSVIT, DANYLO ANDRIIOVYCH, and OPHELIA (a girl wearing yellow and blue). Everyone is looking at their own smartphone.

ELEONORA

(*an anxious woman of rarified beauty*)
> Artem, hello! Hello, Artem! Fuck, what a shitty signal! (*She raises the iPhone trying to get a signal.*) C'mon! Hello! Oh, finally!

ARTEM *appears on the main screen.*

ARTEM
> I can hear you again, love. How are doing over there?

ELEONORA

(*yelling*)
> Are you kidding? For three weeks, there has been no electricity or internet, and there's a mobile connection only in the morning and only in the woods! The only available water comes from the well! None of the stores are open...

ARTEM
> But we had some food stored away...

ELEONORA
> The pharmacies are closed! There are no sanitary pads, Artem. There is no place to get fucking sanitary pads! And there is shooting every hour! They are constantly shelling, pounding and pounding, and then they pound again—and it feels like they'll end up killing us! When will you get me out of here?! Artem, are you a man or just a fucking moron?

ARTEM

Don't you understand what I'm saying? Right now there is no way to get to where you are! I've tried three times in just the past week! Three times! And each and every time I was stopped at our guys' roadblock! There are brutal battles going on there, there are mines, artillery and tanks. We can't get there, love, there is no way to do it. We're going to have to wait.

ELEONORA
(*after a pause with a quiet hopelessness*)

We did try so hard to make this happen. And now it's happened. Artem—I'm pregnant. To be honest with you, I'm very scared. Somewhere inside of me, there now lives a little Ukrainian boy or girl. I don't even know. It's so tiny there inside me while I'm here, in Blyzhni Sady. What kind of a fucking mom I am... Why the hell did I come here?! What an idiot! Why didn't I listen to you! But, you know what, we're going to name her Ksenia, after my mother, okay? And, if it's a boy, then Artem, like you. Just get over here, my dear! Get the fuck over here, please! You've got to get me out of here! I beg you, Artem, I'm losing my mind! I'm losing it! Losing it! Every day I sense that I'm losing it! I'm graying. I pee a hundred times a night from a UTI and from fear. And I'm pregnant, I tell you. On top of all this—I'm pregnant!

ARTEM

When did this happen?

ELEONORA

I took the test the day before yesterday. You know, I always have it on me.

ARTEM

I'll come get you! I will! We just have to wait a little. They say that evacuation corridors are now being set up out of Bucha and Borodianka. If they become accessible, then that means help will come to you, too...

ELEONORA

Artem, stop talking bullshit. Stop it, goddam it! Nobody has any need for us. Borodianka, Bucha, at least they exist on a map. You understand? They are actual cities, but what the hell are we? Not a proper settlement but a completely non-sensical entity. Nobody comes here. We exist neither for the authorities nor for the volunteers. We shouldn't be here. We all should have lived somewhere else. Do you know what I mean?

ARTEM

You know very well that I needed to take care of my business matters.

ELEONORA

I know. You're always taking care of business matters. But these seven years I couldn't get pregnant, and, after every period, I drank for two-three days. We had tickets to Berlin for February 15. You said that you couldn't go because you had business matters, that Berlin and Vienna would have to wait until fall. And I was so hoping to see Bruegel in Vienna. And the Ishtar Gate in Berlin. You were taking care of business matters, so I got offended and organized a ladies' night. On February 24, I woke up alone in a two-story house. I lit up a cigarette and went outside. And it was so warm, so spring-like. While walking, I looked up and saw the Mother of God in the sky, and she was looking at me and crying.

ARTEM
The Mother of God!?

ELEONORA
(*sits down on the pine tree stump next to Danylo Andriiovych*)
Excuse me, I'm going to sit down next to you.

DANYLO ANDRIIOVYCH
That's fine, have a seat.

ELEONORA
I'll explain everything to you in a second, Artem. You understand, when a woman cannot get pregnant for years, especially in our patriarchal society, she begins to feel like a pariah.

ARTEM
Like a what?

KOLIA KHROMYI
Yes, we are slaves, the world's worst! The fellahin and pariahs more fortunate have been,

for they have minds, and complete thoughts,
while for us the Titan's fire still burns within.[12]

ELEONORA
(*to Kolia*)
Thank you. (*To Artem, on the phone*) Pariahs
are what people of a low class are called, like
garbage about which a proper person doesn't
care to talk or even think.

ARTEM
You're exaggerating, as always.

ELEONORA
Yes, damnit, I'm exaggerating. And then there's
your mother who, for these eight years, has been
advising you to dump me with all the clarity
and precision of Rene Descartes. Regardless, a
woman who cannot get pregnant, a pariah of
sorts, she takes various paths before she turns to
the Mother of God. You know, Artem, the Virgin
Mary. If you wanna know who God is, you'll
have to look it up in Wikipedia on your own.

ARTEM
I know who God is.

ELEONORA
So then. Once she's bugged all of the doctors to
death, she decides to turn to the Mother of God.
She goes to Tel-Aviv with her girlfriends to, it
seems, have a good time. That, at least, is what
her husband thinks. But, actually, she hasn't had

a drop of alcohol for a whole month. She tells her girlfriends to fuck off, right there in the Ben Gurion airport, and goes straight to Nazareth to the Catholic Church of the Annunciation, Basilica Annuntiationis. Do you get it?

ARTEM

This was last year, for your birthday?

ELEONORA

Yes, love, on my birthday. And now it's almost a year later. This pariah doesn't get European museums for her birthday and goes with her girlfriends for a couple of days to a cottage compound that is located between Bucha and Borodianka. And, suddenly, the war begins. And, in a few weeks, she realizes that she is pregnant...

ARTEM

I didn't know...

ELEONORA

On the day that the war began I went out, like I said, on our cottage road and there, in the sky, above the Horiana river, above the pine trees, above the pine forest the Mother of God cried. And although I have mostly forgotten about the icons in the Catholic Church of the Annunciation, I suddenly saw them in front of me in astonishing clarity. All of them at once. And, you know, I became so uplifted and light-headed. I began crying and lost consciousness. And, you know what, (*laughing*) I fell down right by Stepan Hryhorovych's gate. Like a complete idiot. He's the one who led me back home.

ARTEM
My poor Elia, my poor girl...

ELEONORA
And that's it, Artem. My head is starting to hurt, I'm feeling nauseous. (*She quietly sighs, laughs, and grabs her head.*) I'm heading home. It took me forty minutes to find a signal today. You get that, Artem? Forty minutes! And my chargers are only good for four days. If nobody lets me plug into the generator. And everyone's supply of gasoline is running low, so that won't be an option much longer. Alright, I'm going. (*She places her iPhone into her pocket and slowly goes towards the gates of the co-op compound*).

ARTEM
Elia, honey, hello! Elia, can you hear me?! Elia!!! (*He looks at the phone and says quietly and seriously*) Elia, I'll try. I'll do everything that I can.

SERAPHYMA'S HUSBAND and her two sons, one five years old and the other seven years old, appear in the conversation window.

SERAPHYMA'S HUSBAND
(*talking into the phone*)
So is she doing better?

SERAPHYMA

She had another episode yesterday. But what's the point of talking about it. We don't have the necessary medicine. And there's no way to get it. At night, I sit next to her holding her hand. I tell her, Mom, as soon as the war is over, I'll make you move to Kyiv and, for the first time in years, you'll get a full medical exam. And she says—no, this is where your father and I have lived lately, and this is where I'll die.

SERAPHYMA'S HUSBAND
(*barely able to contain himself*)

What does this have to do with our kids?! If it wasn't for her, then you'd be with us right now! With me and our kids! Every day, they ask me about you. Every single day! And she'd be ailing in her own apartment in Kyiv now and not in this fucking forest! But what's the point... (*He waves his hand.*)

SERAPHYMA

Don't say anything, that's my mother you're talking about!

SERAPHYMA'S HUSBAND

Fine. I'm giving the phone to our sons. They got up early today so they could talk to you.

SERAPHYMA'S SON

Hey, mom! Dad says you're in the forest with grandma. Serhii, Alisa, and I miss you.

SERAPHYMA

Hello there, my sunshine! I miss you, too! Listen to your father! Listen to grandma and grandpa! Look after your sister! She's younger than you. You need to take care of her.

SERAPHYMA'S SON

We do take care of her.

SERAPHYMA'S OTHER SON

We sing "Hey, I Had a Horse" to her and "Oh, the Red Viburnum."

SERAPHYMA

Does she like it?

SERAPHYMA'S SON

She does, but it makes her cry because we sing too loud.

SERAPHYMA'S OTHER SON

She is afraid of us.

SERAPHYMA'S SON

It's because she's still so little and doesn't understand anything.

SERAPHYMA

But, on the other hand, the two of you are so grown up. So good, so smart. Hello! Hello! (*She looks at the smartphone screen in despair.*) Oh no! No-no-no, don't disappear! Hello!

INNA

(*a young woman with a small dog*)
Mom, you need to go down into the metro, Mom, go down there! Don't stay at home when you hear the air sirens!

INNA'S MOTHER

(*on that very same stool in that very same kitchen*)
I've gotten so tired of running to the metro, Inna. I'm tired. I'm not running anywhere anymore. If I get hit, I get hit. If the Russians feel a need to kill me, then let them kill me. Maybe they'll finally calm down after that?

INNA

Mom, what are you saying! What are you saying!

INNA'S MOTHER

I'm tired of running, I say. Let them kill me. There was a time for living, and now it's time to die.

MAR'IANA

(*quietly*)
Ostap, I don't understand. You're a soldier? How come you just suddenly...

OSTAP

(*on the screen, in a military uniform and smiling*)
Because there's a war out there. Somebody has got to do it. I'm not going to just sit around on Dad's couch and drink beer.

MAR'IANA
Oh Lord! Do you already know where you'll go?
Will you be able to call me?

OSTAP
I'll try to get in touch but, perhaps, not every
day. Don't get upset. I'll leave keys to the
apartment with the neighbors in thirty-eight,
with Stiopa and Valiera.

MAR'IANA
How are they?

OSTAP
For Valiera, not so good. Her entire family is
in Moscow. She spoke with her parents on the
evening of the 24th. She realized that they fully
support Putin. She had a heart attack. Now she
just lies down all the time and barely gets up.
And Stiopa? He's okay, he takes care of her. He
says that, if not for his wife, he'd join me in the
Armed Forces of Ukraine.

MAR'IANA
How's Kyiv?

OSTAP
It's the City of Heroes.

LIUBOV PAVLIVNA
(*a plump, tidy old lady*)
And how's Barsyk doing?

PAVLYK

He's fine. He eats and shits. Nothing new. As for me,
Liuba, I can't sleep without you. You understand?
Every night, I keep checking whether you are next to
me. Three times a night. Your half of the bed is cold.
Your half of my life is empty. You're just not there,
just not there. And the siren just continues to wail.

LIUBOV PAVLIVNA
(*quietly, so that her husband can't hear, wiping her
tears with her index finger*)

Frequent air sirens? Do you go down to the
bomb shelter?

PAVLYK

At first, I went—maybe three times. But now
I only go when I'm very lonely. I go to look at
people. Good people. Younger and older, and
kids, and women. There are so many of us—
Ukrainians—under the fire of these rockets. And
no one understands why Russia is doing this.
What need do the Russians have for all of this...

*Pavlyk says something but it cannot be heard because
of the sound of air sirens in the background. He yells
something and then disappears from the screen.*

LIUBOV PAVLIVNA
(*pensively*)

I miss you so much, and Kyiv, too... Indeed, why
are the Russians doing this?! What's the point?
Hello, Pavlyk! Can you hear me?! Hello? (*She
looks at her phone.*) The signal's gone.

VIKTOR
(*to Liubov Pavlivna*)
    They want to end themselves.

LIUBOV PAVLIVNA
    Excuse me?

VIKTOR
    You asked why the Russians were doing this. And
    I'm answering you—they want to end themselves.

LIUBOV PAVLIVNA
    But how is that possible? They always said—
    we're brothers. And now rockets fall upon
    civilians. Today, I managed to speak with a
    girlfriend that was evacuated from Bucha.
    An utter horror. What she witnessed there is
    difficult to fathom. The Russians are shooting
    up kindergartens, schools, stores, churches, and
    museums. They are raping and stealing. They are
    firing at multi-storied residential buildings with
    machine guns. They're shooting unarmed people
    on the street, just like that. How is this possible?
    Who are these people?

VIKTOR'S FATHER appears on the screen.

VIKTOR'S FATHER
(*he speaks on the screen in front of a yellow-blue
background, addressing Liubov Pavlivna directly*)
    I'll tell you this, Liubov Pavlivna. I myself am a
    Russian. I was born in Tambov. I died in Kharkiv.
    I fished in the Lopan and Tsna rivers. After my

army service, I stayed in Ukraine. I got married, I was happy. I was killed almost simultaneously with the parents of Mar'iana who lives here in the cottage compound, on 12 Lisova Street. I'm actually ashamed that I'm Russian. And that I learned the Ukrainian language only after I died.

LIUBOV PAVLIVNA
(*with interest*)
How is that you say that you've died while I'm talking with you? And without a phone.

VIKTOR'S FATHER
A telephone is not necessary for true conversations.

HRYHORII
Finally! Two bars! Kostiantyn, hello, how is Kyiv doing?!! Hey pal! How's the capital?! Can you hear me? Can you hear?!!

KOSTIANTYN
Yes, Hryhorii, I can hear you! Everything's fine. The capital is holding up. We're holding up. We will not give up our Kyiv! They can't kill all of us!

SERHII
(*with a cigarette in the corner of his mouth*)
Hey, Halia! Why aren't you picking up the phone? You're busy? With what? Hello, Halia, can you hear me? You hear? It's nothing, I just want to know what's going on. I haven't been able to get through for a week and, when I do get through, you don't pick up the phone. How

are you guys doing? How's Ivano-Frankivsk?
How's Auntie Elza doing? Hello, Halia! Hello!
What's going on? I keep losing the signal...
(*He turns to Ophelia.*) She doesn't love me.

OPHELIA

No, she doesn't, Serhii, but that's good. (*She sings.*)

Tomorrow is Saint Valentine's Day,
All in the morning betime,
And I, a maid at your window,
To be your Valentine.
Then up he rose, and donned his clothes,
And dupped the chamber door,
Let in the maid, that out a maid
Never departed more.[13]

SERHII

I was not her first. And won't be her last.

OPHELIA

Understood. But she will be your first and only.

Serhii hides his tears. Music sounds. The artillery is pounding harder and harder, the buzzing of planes can be heard.

An explosion. The lights fade.

SCENE TWO

*On tree stumps that have been toppled by a storm sit
SERHII, MARIIA TSVIT, OLENA VOLODYMYRIVNA,
STEPAN HRYHOROVYCH, KOLIA KHROMYI, VASIA
TSVIT, DANYLO ANDRIIOVYCH, and OPHELIA (a girl
wearing yellow and blue). Everyone is looking at their own
smartphone.*

By Serhii's feet is a half-empty bottle and two shot glasses.

SERHII
What I'm thinking about, Stepan Hryhorovych,
is whether the war will end by summertime.

STEPAN HRYHOROVYCH
It all depends which summer you have in mind.
If you mean the upcoming one, then probably
not. It doesn't look like it. Our guys are fighting
for Kyiv. We're far away from victory.

OLENA VOLODYMYRIVNA
And why are you drinking, Serhii?

MARIIA TSVIT
You should take care of yourself. It's not good
for you!

DANYLO ANDRIOVYCH

It's because Halia is so pampered. She's had a lover in Frankivsk for a long time, and Serhii knows about it. One guy is with her, and do you think the other won't get killed? Halia is twenty-eight, he's fifty-three. Serhii always knew it could happen.

VASIA TSVIT

I see. A quarter of a century difference. Obviously, it will be a problem...

SERHII
(*perplexed*)

And how do you know about the quarter of a century?

VASIA TSVIT

What are you talking about?

SERHII

Well, you just said that there was a quarter century difference.

VASIA TSVIT

Why aren't you taking a bite of something after you do a shot?

SERHII
(*sighing*)

These explosions sober you up before you even manage to get a buzz. So what's the point?

VASIA TSVIT

To feel good. To not get drunk so fast. To keep your wits.

SERHII

What do I need my wits for? (*He pours two shots.*) Anybody want to join? Well, whatever you say. (*He drinks one after the other.*) To Ukraine. To you, Halia.

STEPAN HRYHOROVYCH

By the way, these vegetables that we brought today are all that we could get. They won't give us any more. And there's no reason to ask them. That's it, end of story.

VASIA TSVIT

It's understandable. The people in the villages are probably afraid that, in a few months, there won't be enough food for their own families. And no one knows if they'll be able to plant anything, if there will be a harvest, or, in general, what is to come.

OLENA VOLODYMYRIVNA

So, we have nothing to depend on now.

STEPAN HRYHOROVYCH

The war is dragging on. There are Russians all around, and shootings, and there are no deliveries... And the stench, Serhii, from that moonshine is simply awful. Where did you get it? At Pobieda, from the Kotyks?

KOLIA KHROMYI

You drank moonshine from a flask, and now you sleep by a tub in filth, while somewhere there are pigeons, mansards, poets, the sun, and Paris![14]

SERHII

Yep, we did Paris. I took her everywhere. Of course, I did. And Vasia was correct—twenty-five years. There is a quarter century between us. She doesn't love me. And never did. (*He laughs bitterly.*) While the money was there, she remained loving but didn't want to have children. And I so wanted to have a son. (*He covers his face with his hands.*) Why am I telling you all of this? How shameful. How embarrassing... And she always had someone in Franyk, I don't know him, but I know that he exists and that there was always some kind of connection between them.

OPHELIA

A spiritual one, perhaps.

KOLIA KHROMYI

They can't hear you, Ophelia. Can't hear or see you.

OPHELIA

Of course, they can't see me—that's because I don't exist.

SERHII

(*bitterly*)

Exactly. That's it, a spiritual connection. I don't want to live. I won't.

OLENA VOLODYMYRIVNA
What are you saying, Serhii?! How can you say that? Have you gone nuts?

VASIA TSVIT
The dude is drunk, talks nonsense.

SERHII
Drunk or not drunk, but my head is gray, like linen. And my body is old. And my heart is tiny and doesn't want to beat anymore.

OPHELIA
Exactly, exactly, exactly. The heart doesn't want to beat anymore. But I need to get to the Horiana. I'll swim and paint the water the color of love. Come, my coach! Good night, ladies, good night. Sweet ladies, good night, good night.[15]

SERHII
Good night, fine lady. She looks just like Halia.

OLENA VOLODYMYRIVNA
With whom are you conversing, Serhii?

OPHELIA
(*laughs, rises, goes to the gates of Blyzhni Sady, and sings*)

> And will he not come again?
> And will he not come again?
> No, no, he is dead,
> Go to thy deathbed,

He never will come again.
His beard as white as snow,
All flaxen was his poll.
He is gone, he is gone,
And we cast away moan.
God ha' mercy on his soul!
And of all Christians' souls,
I pray God. God be wi' ye![16]

KOLIA KHROMYI
(*rising*)
> A naiad, such a naiad. Must go with Ophelia.
> Listen to some songs, catch some fish.

OLENA VOLODYMYRIVNA
> Koliusia, tell Baba Karpa that I'll come over in an
> hour.

SERHII
(*pouring two shots*)
> Anybody wanna join me? (*He drinks one shot after
> the other.*) Glory to Ukraine. This one I drink to
> you, Halia.

STEPAN HRYHOROVYCH
> This morning I counted one hundred and twenty cars.

MARIIA TSVIT
> Did many leave from our co-op?

STEPAN HRYHOROVYCH
> Thirty from ours, forty-five from the Town,
> and there were others, too. Some got out of

Nemishaieve, some, by some miracle, from Borodianka, some from nearby villages. They're driving past me and my eyes well up with tears. A minibus with a child. Signs reading "Children" everywhere. And large white flags wave over the cars. Old people and young go. Everyone who can—gets out.

OLENA VOLODYMYRIVNA

It's a lottery. Somebody gets lucky, somebody doesn't. The day before yesterday, a family from the Town was shot and killed at the checkpoint. But they had set out alone without the convoy. I guess they were in a hurry.

VASIA TSVIT

Are you saying that kids got shot?

STEPAN HRYHOROVYCH

Three adults and three children. Yesterday they were buried at the cemetery near the Town.

MARIIA TSVIT

Oh my God, how horrible! Why did they do this!

STEPAN HRYHOROVYCH

Well, who knows. Something bugged them, I guess.

DANYLO ANDRIIOVYCH

The driver, the family's father, told the Russians that they were occupiers. He couldn't contain himself.

VASIA TSVIT
They executed him over one word?

DANYLO ANDRIIOVYCH
And the Word was with God, and the Word was God.

OLENA VOLODYMYRIVNA
For one word, or two, who knows. They don't need a reason, Vasia.

STEPAN HRYHOROVYCH
The cream of the crop is leaving. The smart, attentive ones, with cars and money. There's almost nobody left in the Town's territorial defense forces. Most of the capable guys left, and those that remained are useless.

OLENA VOLODYMYRIVNA
Today, my acquaintances told me that there are problems in the Town. The local hooligans are pilfering the abandoned homes. The alcoholics and the druggies have come out. And who's going to knock them back in their place? There are no rules in the occupied territories.

MARIIA TSVIT
What about the police?

OLENA VOLODYMYRIVNA
There are no police, either. Maybe they've scattered or gone to Kyiv. While the territorial defense was still there, some sense of order

prevailed. But now, I think difficult times have
arrived.

SERHII
Looting the Town will occupy them for the next
month or so, and then they will go after the cottages.

STEPAN HRYHOROVYCH
Anything is possible. And it's our riffraff, our
people. At least they won't kill anyone. But,
soon, the Russians will come here. All the
villages surrounding us are occupied. And that's
a real horror.

MARIIA TSVIT
What's wrong with us, Vasia? What are we,
cursed?! We left Donetsk thinking we'd settle
here somehow and have a life. But Russians have
now come here, too. They've come and ruined
our lives again. Why is that, Vasia? Why?!

VASIA TSVIT
Stop it, Mariia, please, I'm begging you.

MARIIA TSVIT
But I haven't said anything, Vasia, it's just that
everything that is to take place is hard for me to
face.

VASIA TSVIT
Rhyming verbs is a bad sign. (*He hugs Mariia and
kisses her head.*) Please stop it, sunshine, there's
no need. You'll just stress your heart.

DANYLO ANDRIIOVYCH
  You and she need to get out of here, Vasia.

VASIA TSVIT
(*upset*)
  Get out of here? How? And go where?

OLENA VOLODYMYRIVNA
  It really is problematic. We spent three days
  trying to get our granddaughter and her three
  kids out of here.

MARIIA TSVIT
  Were they able to do it?

SERHII
(*drinking*)
  Glory to Ukraine! And this one I drink to you, Halia.

OLENA VOLODYMYRIVNA
  Yes, thank God. But we went to the dam for
  three days. There, after seven a.m., cars queue in
  a column that heads for the Russian checkpoint
  and further, if they are lucky, to Rivne.

STEPAN HRYHOROVYCH
  On days that the Russians let people pass
  through the checkpoints, a column of cars forms
  until nine a.m. Another, in the afternoon, from
  around one or two o'clock. After four p.m. they
  usually don't allow anybody to pass through.
  So, we went with our dear ones to those columns
  and asked around.

OLENA VOLODYMYRIVNA

No one would take them. No one. They look at you, drive by slowly and don't take anyone. Even when the car is half-empty.

MARIIA TSVIT

Why?

STEPAN HRYHOROVYCH

People don't have much fuel left. No one knows where they can get a fill-up. Every extra person in the car is an extra waste of fuel. And to get stuck on these roads at night with kids and without fuel or a mobile connection is truly terrifying. Hey, I'm not judging anyone. I get it. Some get out while others must stay behind.

DANYLO ANDRIIOVYCH

Someone dies, while someone else must live on. At that moment, when we are to choose, we don't really choose anything. When that moment comes, it turns out that, suddenly, that choice has been made a long time ago and maybe not even by you. You are left with nothing but to accept it.

OLENA VOLODYMYRIVNA

In the end, we lucked out. Acquaintances of ours were leaving and took our grandkids. But we had to wait for a while.

STEPAN HRYHOROVYCH
For two weeks now, people stand on both sides
of the dam from early in the morning. Some are
in wheelchairs. There are really old people, too.
Some ask those leaving to take their children
with them. It doesn't matter where to, as long
as it's out of this hell. They have no hope that
they'll get out themselves. They stand there
without their things. From morning 'til night.
They beg but people don't take them.

OLENA VOLODYMYRIVNA
The cars with white flags drive slowly along the
dam. There's the wind, the sun, the morning
frost. The yellow reeds and the blue sky above
the lake. You hold a sheet of paper that has
the place you want to go written on it. But the
people in the cars drive away and lower their
faces so as not to look into your eyes.

STEPAN HRYHOROVYCH
Yep, that's how it is...

OLENA VOLODYMYRIVNA
Yesterday, I saw a mother sending off two
children ages five to seven, a boy and a girl.

MARIIA TSVIT
Did anyone pick them up?

OLENA VOLODYMYRIVNA
Some old guy from Pylypovychi pulled over.
Said he's heading to Kyiv and can only take the

kids. But is there anyone in Kyiv to pick them up? Someone from their family or perhaps some acquaintances were found. Telephone numbers were exchanged. She kissed the children. She even gave them a bag with things to take with them. The boy was very uneasy while his little sister grabbed hold of him and wouldn't let him go, even when it was time to get into the car. The mother held it together, tried to cheer them up, calm them, and promised that they would see one another soon. She held it together until the car turned onto the road to Nova Hreblia that led to the initial Russian checkpoint. And then she fell to her knees right there on the road and began to scream. She screamed for her children so much that she passed out.

DANYLO ANDRIIOVYCH
(*to Vasia*)
  Call Kazymyr. Maybe he'll be able to help you.

VASIA TSVIT
  What Kazymyr?

DANYLO ANDRIIOVYCH
  The crow and the student.

VASIA TSVIT
(*with fright*)
  What crow?

DANYLO ANDRIIOVYCH
  Stop it. You know him very well, going back to 2014.

VASIA TSVIT

I don't know what you are talking about! I don't know, and I don't want to know!

MARIIA TSVIT

With whom are you speaking, Vasia?

Vasia Tsvit gets up and pretends that he is catching a signal. Mariia Tsvit carefully observes him. Danylo Andriiovych walks along with Vasia.

DANYLO ANDRIIOVYCH

He's the one who saved you and your family. He's that crow. Remember?

VASIA TSVIT

There's no signal.

DANYLO ANDRIIOVYCH

There may be no signal, but there definitely was, and is, a crow. Your trusted student, Kazymyr. That spring, he saved our lives. Recall the spring of 2014. Terrible rains. Horrific and beautiful storms. The sky was a fiery yellow and red. It thundered and circled. And slammed, like now. Pleasant and terrifying.

VASIA TSVIT

In spring of 2014, in Donetsk, a huge number of all kinds of ants, insects, mice, snails and rats appeared. I was delivering lessons online, writing something, staying up, working late. And, on my windowsill, a crow appeared. A large, black one with a blue sheen. A true raven, Corvus corax. And then he began accompanying me on my way to my lessons and morning jogs, remember Mariia, I kept telling you about him?

MARIIA TSVIT
Why are you recalling this all of a sudden?

VASIA TSVIT
I thought of it for some reason. If it weren't for him, we wouldn't have left in time. Thanks to him, we remained alive.

STEPAN HRYHOROVYCH
And the sun is noticeably warming, and the cold is not so intense anymore. And see, in the afternoon, the temperature is already above freezing. But, after two, I feel like going home. (*Laughing*) I'm old, my blood doesn't warm up anymore. I guess, I'll go, too. Shall we go, dear wife?

OLENA VOLODYMYRIVNA
Yes, Stepan.

MARIIA TSVIT
(*standing up*)
Vasia, that's it, we need to go, too. I'm cold, it's time to make dinner, and you promised to read Shakespeare to me. Let's go before it gets dark.

VASIA TSVIT
Yeah, you're right. Let's go home. All these years, I walk in the forest just breathing it in

or, for example, foraging mushrooms, or simply looking at the snow and I think: "I want to go home." And, in that very moment, I understand that there is no home. We don't have a home. We don't. And probably never will.

OLENA VOLODYMYRIVNA
These days, Vasia, half of Ukraine is being left without a home. So, you're not alone.

SERHII
The last one is to Ukraine.

He drinks the shot. An explosion. The lights fade.

The artillery is pounding, the buzzing of planes can be heard.

SCENE THREE

The bedroom in the Tsvit home. The ticking of the clock can be heard. The noise made by the furnace can be heard. From regular explosions, the dishware in the china cabinet occasionally rings. We can't see the whole room across the stage because the windows are covered with a thick black cloth. By one of the windows, DANYLO ANDRIIOVYCH sits on a stool and reads something. In the opposite corner, sitting on a dilapidated sofa is a strange creature: KAZYMYR—a person with the giant head of a Corvus corax.

MARIIA puts on her night clothes. She grabs her own flashlight and sits down on the bed with it.

MARIIA TSVIT
(to the audience)
> He was always a bit strange. We met at the publisher's office. I worked there as an editor, and he brought in his manuscript. And he seemed so funny to me, so nice, that I fell in love with him at first glance. We got married right before the war started. You won't believe it—we went to the marriage registration office on February 24, 2014. And within a few months, the Russian soldiers entered Donetsk. We were forced to drop everything and leave Donetsk. And eight years

later, right on the anniversary of our wedding, the full-blown Russian invasion began. My husband and I were so looking forward to our anniversary, we were so looking forward to our celebration...

The door slams shut. VASIA TSVIT enters wearing only his briefs.

VASIA TSVIT
Man is it cold! Who are you talking with?

MARIIA TSVIT
With no one. (*She quickly slides under several comforters that are stacked one upon another.*) For some reason, I'm recalling how we met, started dating, and how you took me to the marriage registration office.

VASIA TSVIT
There's nothing to recall. Stepan Hryhorovych was right on—they're bombing today like never before. Maybe it's the Russian heavy artillery that was set up at the dam. I know I shouldn't curse but that's the only way I can address them. Damn Russia, damn, damn it. Be damned for eternity. We are not forgiving them now nor will we ever forgive them. (*He shakes his head and pauses.*) Where's my goddamn night outfit?

He rushes to put on his night clothes. He purposefully does this in a very comical manner in order to cheer up his wife, almost falling down several times while doing it. Mariia Tsvit finally smiles.

VASIA TSVIT
It is so cold! Why is it so cold?! It's already March, but we can't warm up at all. God forbid the Russians damage our gas line. What will we do then, dear wife? It's five degrees outside. But it's weird. In the afternoon it's in the forties. Whereas at night it is so cold that it's impossible to heat up the house.

MARIIA TSVIT
What will we talk about?

VASIA TSVIT
(*dressed, slides under his own three thick comforters*)
About birds.

MARIIA TSVIT
About birds?

VASIA TSVIT
Yes, about birds. When we were out in the meadow and I mentioned Kazymyr, you became uncomfortable for some reason.

MARIIA TSVIT
You know why. You made all of that up back then.

VASIA TSVIT
I know, I know. You didn't believe me then, and you don't believe me now.

MARIIA TSVIT
In those days, we were all in a state of shock not much less than we are today. You have a subtle

nature. It's not that you made him up. It's just that you saw your own intuition in the image of a crow, a made-up one, or maybe one you actually saw. You are a writer, after all, and you have a special imagination and sensitivity.

VASIA TSVIT
I'll tell you again, it was Kazymyr who gave me the date by which we needed to leave Donetsk if we hoped to remain alive.

MARIIA TSVIT
(*irritated*)
Don't give a crow a human name! I don't want to hear any more about this! What, now you're going to tell me about Danylo Andriiovych, too?!

VASIA TSVIT
I will indeed. Danylo Andriiovych was the only one from his Belarusian-Ukrainian family to have survived the Holodomor. He was very wise but didn't pursue studies because, in Donetsk, they were conducted exclusively in Russian. But he refused. He spoke exclusively in Ukrainian until the day he died. That is why his whole life his employment was restricted to menial labor at the rail depot. Throughout his life, Danylo Andriiovych watched how his son became a Russian engineer, how we, his grandkids, spoke only in Russian and didn't remember anything about the history of our family, how we reiterated what we heard at playgrounds, schools, and universities. A mechanical genius,

which is why they kept him at the depot, he could fix any mechanism, could sense how a motor functioned from a distance, and knew many jokes and various stories. During the week, he was a clean, quiet, smiling drunk, whom nobody took seriously. On Saturdays and Sundays, he was a sorrowful, often dirty man whose eyes had been blinded by a grief that had a source unknown to anyone. He wasn't invited over to our place very often. Whenever he did come over, he always brought flowers for my mother. And he would say, "For the lady." This seemed to annoy father. Danylo Andriiovych and Kazymyr—they are the source of my transformation. If you are interested. He is the one who led me to my memory and to my Ukraine when 2014 arrived.

There is a pause. Danylo Andriiovych gets up and, putting his hand on his back, walks up to the bed. He bends over toward Mariia, nudges the comforter and tenderly touches her hair. She reflexively squints and smiles.

DANYLO ANDRIIOVYCH
Today I listened how you recited Shakespeare to her, very clearly—well done. Me, on the other hand, I've spent the whole evening musing about Myhail´ Semenko's "Manifest of Kvero-Futurism." That's a really cool text. What do you think? That Semenko sure does say some spot-on things about the coexistence of the national and the universal. In other words, the ontological space and everyday empiricism. (*He sits down on the floor by the bed.*)

VASIA TSVIT
(*trying not to look at Danylo Andriiovych*)
  I can tell you about Semenko's "Manifest."
  So as not to fall asleep. Well, you remember
  Semenko, don't you? He is a theoretician of
  Ukrainian Futurism, Ukrainian poetry, urban
  topics, the Executed Renaissance. He was a
  funny and cool dude.

MARIIA TSVIT
(*raising her shoulders*)
  You only read him to me once in the past,
  I don't remember anything. It's all very hazy and
  unclear.   .

VASIA TSVIT
  Everything is clear in it, and it's easy to
  remember. The main thing in his manifest—self-
  existent things.

MARIIA TSVIT
  What kinds of things?

VASIA TSVIT
  Self-existent. What a wonderful word it is!
  I'm not sure what Semenko had in mind with
  that concept. (*He laughs.*) But I can tell you
  how I see it. Self-existent things are things
  that are founded upon themselves. I think that
  Semenko got this from Bergson, that is, from
  Kant, Descartes, in other words—the Socratic
  philosophical line. He has in mind that there are
  certain things such as conscience, goodness,

beauty. They are not founded upon anything, you understand? They contain their origin within them. They exist because they exist. For example, what is conscience based on? On conscience! On itself. It is the undeniable and only base for itself. You understand? This is classic Kantian tautology. It's a rule because it's a rule. It is goodness because it is goodness.

MARIIA TSVIT
It is Ukraine because it is Ukraine.

VASIA TSVIT
(*with joyful bewilderment*)
Yes, Mariia, exactly! Ukraine because it is Ukraine!

DANYLO ANDRIIOVYCH
She's a wise woman. Picks up everything quickly.

VASIA TSVIT
Yes, of course, Ukraine is as valuable a thing as conscience. It, like conscience, is not measured against those things that appear in the world. Neither by a government, nor a parliament, nor even by certain aides to the president. It is a foundation for itself in our hearts and in our lives. Like that Kyiv bird that always hovers in the sky over the dam. I've seen it for all these years that we've lived here, but you don't trust my eyes.

A *few explosions from which the dishware rings and something falls down in the china cabinet.*

MARIIA TSVIT
Oh my God!

VASIA TSVIT
That one was really close to us. (*He gets up, walks up to the window, and pushes away the black cloth.*) Mariia, that landed in the neighboring co-op. Across the lake. Exactly eight hundred and seventy yards from here. It looks like homes are burning there. What should we do?

MARIIA TSVIT
Nothing.

VASIA TSVIT
Maybe we should try heading over there, what do you think? Although it will take about an hour if we go along the road. And their gate, like ours, is probably locked overnight.

MARIIA TSVIT
Yes, their gate is locked. And they let their dogs roam at night. And, at night, it will take an hour going along the road on which a Russian armored personnel vehicle is driving. You won't go. Not over my dead body, Vasia. Stay home, for God's sake!

VASIA TSVIT
But what if someone there needs help?!

MARIIA TSVIT
(*yelling*)
> I need your help, Vasia, I need it! I'll lose my mind if you leave the house at night and go for three miles in the dark and without a phone connection! If you are needed, the guys from the territorial defense will come get you. Stay put! Let your Danylo Andriiovych go there instead!

DANYLO ANDRIIOVYCH
(*turning the pages of the Bible*)
> What, I'm supposed to just drop everything and go? Well, it looks like you've found yourselves a sucker for this.

MARIIA TSVIT
> Listen, there should be some wine left over from our so-called anniversary. Let's crack open a bottle, Vasia. It's so hard for me, so hard. Maybe it will offer a bit of relief?

VASIA TSVIT
> You know me, I'm game.

He turns on his flashlight, gets up, and walks out. He returns a minute later with a bottle and two wine glasses. He fills them with wine and gives Mariia a glass. They drink.

VASIA TSVIT
> A few bottles remain. Let's leave them for an extreme situation. No one knows how much longer we'll be here. We survive like birds of the air, I tell you. And we don't even know on what.

MARIIA TSVIT

Birds of the air, you say? That's appropriate. It's so spot on that you've hit the bull's eye. (*She leans in next to her husband and looks into his eyes.*) And now, be honest with me, Vasia—why did you bring up that huge crow today, the one that never flew up to you and that never lived in our mansard, and that never drank port wine with you, did not fly above your head all of March and April 2014, never yelled "it's war, run with your wife to the Dnipro and its ramparts, so you can see and hear how the river roars"[17] in three different languages? Who, even taking into account that he knew Ukrainian, could not know for sure that, a few months after our move to Kyiv, a missile would destroy our apartment on the Donetsk outskirts. And that non-existent crow could not have been your student because birds, especially as big as that, are not allowed into the university lecture halls.

Kazymyr gets up from the couch.

KAZYMYR

I didn't live in the mansard, she's right about that. And I wasn't present at the class meetings. Vasia is exaggerating there, that's for sure. He's in the humanities. They have such great imaginations—you and I wish we had such. But you must understand that we, birds, exist in order to act as road signs for all those who run along the trails of the city park, and for those who don't. For those who walk in the darkness,

gazing into the stormy Donbas sky, and for
those who simply look through a window.
For those who see dreams in which a nuclear
war begins and for those who don't see such
dreams. (*He walks up to* Vasia, *who looks at him
with sad eyes.*) Tell her, Vasia, tell her the truth.
Tell her—there he is, that crow, standing in
front of me. Tall, skinny, with something akin
to a crow's head for a head, while everyone
understands that it is just a mask that decorates
or symbolizes something.

DANYLO ANDRIIOVYCH
(*to Kazymyr*)
Sit down next to me. No one is pouring anything
for us here, but they're not chasing us away either.

VASIA TSVIT
(*to Mariia*)
What does a crow symbolize?

MARIIA TSVIT
Well, how should I know? You tell me!

VASIA TSVIT
An intermediary between heaven and earth.
In fact, over these eight years that we've
lived here, he would bring me news about my
parents who stayed behind in Donetsk. And
it's true, Kazymyr is my student and my crow,
self-existent like conscience, unfathomable like
death, he's present here and now. Together with
my grandfather, Danylo Andriiovych. They're

sitting next to us, upset that they can't drink wine with us.

MARIIA TSVIT
(*laughing*)
Stop making fun of me, Vasia.

VASIA TSVIT
You know that I spoke with my father twice a year. My mother and I have not spoken for six years. And he told me everything. How, for the first few years, they couldn't forgive me for forsaking my native city and for choosing Ukraine. And how they began to quickly age, fall ill, and forget when and why this all began. I still cannot fathom how such changes can happen with people so quickly. I cannot believe it. Do you know that my mother has been bedridden for almost a year now? She has to crawl to the bathroom. Did you know that?

MARIIA TSVIT
(*caresses his head*)
My dear Vasia, Vasylko...

VASIA TSVIT
That my father doesn't remember anything anymore. About me nor about my attitude toward Russia. Not about his own, for that matter. Not to mention the reasons for this war. He goes out of his home and only sees its results. And he is baffled every time. He can't comperehend how what has happened is even possible. Somehow,

he is able to take care of their needs. Sometimes, he even reads and watches TV. And mom, can you believe it, asks, every morning, "Where's my Vasia?" Did you know that, dear wife of mine? She asks, "Where is my Vasia?!" While Vasia, damn it, is here, near Kyiv, picking mushrooms now for eight years in a row. Picking mushrooms until he can't anymore. The Polish mushroom has replaced my blood and my lymphatic fluid. Did you know that? Your husband is a mushroom hunter. A writer of self-existent Ukraine. A fan of Semenko and Domontovych, a.k.a. Petrov. While my mom wakes up in the morning, looks at her husband, my dad, and asks: where is my son and why iisn't he here with us? (*He cries.*)

MARIIA TSVIT

Oh God, Vasia, but you cannot know this for sure!

VASIA TSVIT

I know all of this for sure. And I cannot return there. Because what they'll do to me is worse than what they did with Kolia Khromyi.

MARIIA TSVIT

My dear Vasia, Vasylko...

VASIA TSVIT

And now we have this. He flew over here, my crow, my Kazymyr. He's here right now. Don't be afraid. They're with us, both grandpa and the crow. They are dear to us. I think all of this has a very important meaning. A heavenly sign. I'm sure of it, Mariia, I understand everything. We just need to survive. I uncorked this bottle and thought of how nice it is that we have a lot of wine. There is something celebratory in that. It's a good sign. True, there isn't much bread, but there's enough wine. We were expecting guests. We planned on celebrating our anniversary for three days, having fun and making love. We bought all of this food for our anniversary, seafood and fish, olives and cheese.

MARIIA TSVIT
(*almost calmly, although tears stream down her cheeks*)
We already finished off the cheese.

VASIA TSVIT
Who would've thought that the invasion would begin on our anniversary.

MARIIA TSVIT
No one did. And don't be sad. The wine and olives won't disappear. We'll find a way to invite our co-op friends over. (*She lifts the wine glass.*) Here's to you, my love! (*She laughs.*) Say hello to Kazymyr and to your grandpa! Too bad they don't drink. Mother of God, please look after us all!

DANYLO ANDRIIOVYCH
And greetings to you, Mariia.

An explosion. The lights fade. The dishware rings in the cabinet.

ACT THREE

SCENE ONE

A frigid morning. Explosions and smoke. A pine forest, a meadow, the sun, snow. In the meadow, around thirty people with smartphones and cell phones in their hands are catching a mobile signal, they converse but their conversations are almost inaudible. On the background screen, fifteen to twenty conversation windows are on: Ukrainian soldiers, adults and children, women and men of various ages. They converse, cry, and laugh.

To the right, on tree stumps that have been toppled by a storm sit MARIIA TSVIT, OLENA VOLODYMYRIVNA, STEPAN HRYHOROVYCH, KOLIA KHROMYI, VASIA TSVIT, DANYLO ANDRIIOVYCH, KAZYMYR, and OPHELIA (wearing yellow and blue). Everyone is looking at their own smartphone. Vasia Tsvit and Mariia Tsvit, disregarding the others, embrace, he whispers something in her ear, she occasionally laughs quietly.

On the main screen at the front of the stage, PAVLYK is in a conversation window. He looks at the forest, at the people who are sitting, and nervously yawns. He picks

*up his phone, dials a number and listens. He places the
phone on the table. He makes himself coffee.*

PAVLYK
I don't understand what's going on in this forest.
Liuba always calls around this time. And never
later. And we had made plans to talk today. She
is so decent and responsible. She always does
what she says she'll do. But there's no reason to
get so upset, no reason.

*SERAPHYMA'S HUSBAND appears on the screen, sits
down on a chair, lights a cigarette.*

SERAPHYMA'S HUSBAND
I love Seraphyma. And, if I occasionally do yell
at her, it's only because of her fucking mother!
Pardon my French, but that's how she is. She
doesn't pity her daughter. And never did... (*He
looks at his wristwatch.*) Perhaps it is she
who is making her late. Maybe she's calling
me now. She realizes how we worry about
her here. The children asked that I remember
everything that their mom says, so that I can
tell them later.

PAVLYK
How old are your kids?

SERAPHYMA'S HUSBAND
The girl is three. The boys are seven and five.
They're great kids. But they don't want to accept
the fact that they only have their grandma and

dad near them. They really miss Seraphyma. Every day, it needs to be explained to them why their mother is not with them. I still don't know how to explain to children what a war is, and why Russia is doing what it is doing.

PAVLYK

There's been no contact with Liuba for a while. And my heart is aching. What's going on?

ELEONORA
(*attempting to dial up Artem*)

I've got a signal. Three whole bars! The call is getting through. I can hear it getting through. But he's not picking up the phone. I know that there's no fucking way that's possible! This cannot be! This is fucked up! What am I—just some random bitch?! How is this possible. Why did I come here?! Why didn't I stay with him?!

On that screen, on that very stool, in that same kitchen, appears INNA'S MOTHER.

INNA'S MOTHER

Guys, have you seen Inna?

PAVLYK

No.

SERAPHYMA'S HUSBAND

We haven't. We can't wait to see our dear ones.

INNA'S MOTHER
(*sighing*)
I barely got any sleep last night. Air sirens.
Something exploding far away. I didn't fall asleep
until the crack of dawn and then Inna came to me.
She said that she really needed some water. And
I told her to drink some. That there was fresh cool
water in this jug. And then she tells me, "No, Mom,
I need living water."[18] Do you understand? She
asked for living water. I woke up in tears. It wasn't
that horrific a dream. But what was that, my Inna
asking for living water? And what is living water?

KOLIA KHROMYI
A ray will flash in muddled thoughts—I await the
rays. I don't want to think, I don't want thought,
a tired thought.[19]

MAR'IANA
Ostap, honey, how are you?

OSTAP
(*with an automatic rifle, standing in front of a dugout*)
We're beating the orcs, sister, as best we can.
And how are you doing?

MAR'IANA
There were a couple of flybys at night at the co-
op. It's so horrific. So horrific. My hands are still
shaking.

OSTAP
The Russians are attacking cottages on purpose?

MAR'IANA

Who knows, maybe on purpose. People died on
the two roads closest to the lake. Good people.
I wasn't friends with any of them, but I saw
them, of course, every day and in the evening,
at meetings, and here in the meadow where
we come to catch the mobile signal. One house
simply collapsed, like a kid's constructor set.
The other burned down. There was a big fire.
Shrapnel cut through the closer cottages. There
are casualties and injured folks.

OSTAP

And you were able to deal with the fire yourselves?

MAR'IANA

No. We called firemen. The guys went to pick
them up in the Town.

OSTAP

And they came over? They're still able to work,
in today's conditions?

MAR'IANA

Yes. They work and save people. They buy gas
with their own money. Risking their lives every
day. If it weren't for them, the fire would have
spread to other streets.

PAVLYK
(*to Seraphyma's Husband*)

Do you hear what she's saying?

SERAPHYMA'S HUSBAND

I do. Oh my God, oh my God! (*He covers his mouth so as not to scream.*)

OSTAP

Take care of yourself.

PAVLYK

Our building is on the street right next to the lake. A hundred yards from the beach.

INNA'S MOTHER

O God, Inna! (*She whispers.*) O God! Living water. (*She puts her hand to her heart and disappears from the screen.*)

MAR'IANA
(*laughing*)

I don't know what that means in these conditions. How am I supposed to take care of myself, Ostap? Well okay, you take care of yourself, too, brother. May the Guardian Angel watch over you.

KOLIA KHROMYI

Listen, love, I lift my hands—listen: there's a rustling... What gesture of those all alone might not be overheard by many things?[20]

SERAPHYMA'S HUSBAND

This cannot be. It just can't. I don't want to believe it. I can't believe it. And what am I to

do now? What do I tell the kids? My love,
Seraphyma, my sunshine, how can it be...

KOLIA KHROMYI
Listen, my love, I close my eyes—this
movement—it accepts your heart? Listen, I look
up again... But why are you not here?[21]

PAVLYK
We lived together for forty-five years. Russians,
why did you kill her? She was funny and
good. Small. She taught Russian language and
literature her whole life. She regarded your
culture highly. She was hoping that there would
be a change of government in the Kremlin and
that a new phase would begin, and so on... And
you went and killed her...

*Explosions, smoke, the sound of helicopters that are flying
low. It begins to sound in the slowed rhythm of Pyotr
Tchaikovsky's "Dance of the Little Swans." Kolia Khromyi,
Ophelia, Kazymyr, and Danylo Andriiovych begin to dance.*

KAZYMYR
Nine people have perished, five of them children,
the youngest was three years old. Four people
who were critically wounded were taken to a
health clinic in the Town. Have you ever been
in the Town? The clinic's a one-story building.
A walnut tree began growing on the porch last
year, and it continues to grow. No one was able
to yank it out. The only medicines they have
are rubbing alcohol and pain relievers. There

isn't a single surgeon there. They, those unlucky cottage dwellers who are still alive, will all pass away in a few hours. They're not going to make it. But at least they won't be in pain. Pain isn't a great companion. It doesn't allow you to see death's true causes and effects clearly.

OPHELIA
It's so nice to dance to Tchaikovsky with fine people in the middle of a Kyiv forest.[22]

DANYLO ANDRIIOVYCH
Kazymyr and I are not people. And it would be a pleasure to dance with you, whether it's to Tchaikovsky or Glinka, because you're so young and so attractive.

KAZYMYR
Well, I prefer twelve-tone music.

(*Schoenberg's* Suite for Piano, Op. 25 *is heard in the background but dies down in the second measure, and then Tchaikovsky is heard again.*)

OPHELIA
I'm four hundred years old, by the way. Looks can be deceiving.

DANYLO ANDRIIOVYCH
I've always liked grown women and that great Russian culture.

KAZYMYR

Their culture is a strange thing. Just as soon
as you come to truly embrace it, here it comes
rolling in on tanks made in the USSR.

DANYLO ANDRIIOVYCH

That's true. This Tchaikovsky sure is a beauty.
If only someone were to read a bit of Pushkin,
too.

OPHELIA

In this forest, you could get a bullet for reading
Pushkin.

KAZYMYR

You're exaggerating, my dear. But I agree, the
trends are very encouraging. And really, it's only
the beginning.

KOLIA KHROMYI

And there will be no thoughts, and phrases will
scatter, and tragically repeat. And no one will
say that this was beautiful, and it will flicker and
fade with no return.[23]

DANYLO ANDRIIOVYCH

You, Kolia, would be better off singing Ukrainian
songs. Because those poems of yours are kind of
getting me depressed.

The music quiets, but the characters continue to dance.

ELEONORA
(*yells*)
> Yes! Artem, my love, I'm here! Hello!

OLEKSANDR, *a gloomy guy in a car, appears on the screen.*

OLEKSANDR
> It's not Artem, I'm sorry.

ELEONORA
> What do you mean, not Artem? Why not Artem? (*She looks at her iPhone.*) That's his number. What's going on? Where is Artem?

OLEKSANDR
> Are you Eleonora?

ELEONORA
> Yes, I'm Eleonora! And who the fuck are you? Why do you have my husband's phone?!

OLEKSANDR
> Your husband was killed today by a mine near a Russian checkpoint. He drove onto a field to avoid a burned-out vehicle on the road and got blown up. The car, strangely, is okay, but he died.

ELEONORA
> And how... How do you know this? Did you see him as he...

OLEKSANDR

We were driving together in two cars. I was heading to the Town, to get my parents. He was ahead of me, going to get you. But he ran into bad luck. I'm sorry about this. But I had to let you know. Forgive me. I wanted, you see, to call you from my own phone but then saw your call on his phone... And decided to answer it.

ELEONORA

I understand. Thank you.

OLEKSANDR

How can I help you?

ELEONORA

You already have. Did you know him for a long time?

OLEKSANDR

I barely knew him. He found me in a group chat among people who have family in the Town.

ELEONORA

Understood.

OLEKSANDR

Please forgive me.

ELEONORA

There is nothing to forgive you for.

OLEKSANDR

I'll send you a text with my contact information. Give me a call when you get out, and I'll give you Artem's belongings. I shouldn't have done it, but I got his body and the things that he had with him. I took a risk.

ELEONORA

I understand. And in what state is he? I mean, his body.

OLEKSANDR

Hello, I can't hear you. I'm saying, he had money on him. A pretty large amount. Hello.

ELEONORA

I'm asking you, what's the deal with his body?! Where will Artem be buried?

OLEKSANDR

Hello. I can't hear anything.

Oleksandr disappears from the screen.

ELEONORA
(*yells*)

I want to know where my husband will be buried! Hello! Hello! Hello, shit! Hello... (*She sits down on the ground, closes her eyes, and remains silent.*)

Pavlyk cries on the screen and lights up a cigarette. Seraphyma's Husband looks to the side, his sons come to him, he hugs them and closes his eyes.

HALIA appears.

HALIA
And where did my little cricket disappear to? Does anybody know? Guys, have you heard anything?

KAZYMYR
He's lying in the health clinic in the Town, dying. His stomach got hit with two pieces of shrapnel. He doesn't yell anymore. He just moans. All night, when he was in great pain, he yelled: "Halia." And, when it let up a bit, he sang. Turns out, he was a courageous guy. That's how it is. And how's Auntie Elza? How's her cholesterol?

DANYLO ANDRIIOVYCH
Won't last long. Neither the cholesterol nor Auntie Elza.

OPHELIA
(*lights up a cigarette*)
Forget about Auntie Elza. Halia's relatives stripped Serhii of everything in five years. Moreover, he saw that they were ripping him off, yet he always wired all of his money to two recipients only. The first, the Come Back Alive foundation. And Halia didn't know about that. And the second, their joint bank account. He left a little bit for himself, but it was so meager that it's not even worth mentioning. He loved that woman too much. Meanwhile, Halia was with her lover every night for the last month. Her parents have no problem with that. It's

very convenient. That's the kind of people they are... Why the hell did you come here, Halia, you fucking asshole?

HALIA

I don't know what you're talking about. What foundation? My Serhii was giving me everything! And, besides, what are you even talking about?

OPHELIA

You know what I'm talking about. He was forty-seven, you're twenty-two. You knew what you were doing. You came to work for his firm, noticed this gray and tired guy, thought about it, and decided you could do it. And you did. Serhii fell in love in a way that only a guy pushing fifty could—a final, hopeless love. He gave you everything, Halia. To you and to your relatives. Your whole fortune—it's his money. All of your happiness, girl—it's his love. And you won't have anything like this ever again in your life. Believe me. I've been walking on this earth for four hundred years now. And I never met Hamlet. Serhii was a human, and you are a cheap, dumb whore, Halia. Believe me, I'm an archetype and a symbol—and you're dumb and cheap.

HALIA

And who are you?! What is going on here?! Where is my husband?!

ELEONORA
(*yelling*)
> Go fuck yourself, you animal. Get out of here, you slut!

Halia disappears.

KOSTIANTYN appears.

KOSTIANTYN
(*in a military uniform, in body armor, with an automatic rifle*)
> Listen, boys and girls. Has anyone seen my brother, Hrysha Perebyinis?

Once again, the explosions grow louder, everyone who is in the meadow dances to "The Dance of the Little Swans."

Explosions. The lights fade.

SCENE TWO

The sun, a somewhat warm temperature, the snow has disappeared. On tree stumps that have been toppled by a storm sit KAZYMYR, ELEONORA, MAR'IANA, MARIIA TSVIT, OLENA VOLODYMYRIVNA, STEPAN HRYHOROVYCH, KOLIA KHROMYI, VASIA TSVIT, DANYLO ANDRIIOVYCH, and OPHELIA (a girl wearing yellow and blue). Everyone is looking at their own smartphone.

STEPAN HRYHOROVYCH
Yesterday, the Russians entered the neighboring co-op on the other side of the lake.

VASIA TSVIT
What for?

STEPAN HRYHOROVYCH
Robbery. Two guys were shot dead.

MARIIA TSVIT
My God, what for?

STEPAN HRYHOROVYCH
They don't need any reasons. They are murderers and rapists.

DANYLO ANDRIIOVYCH
Dead souls.

VASIA TSVIT
I hear that Kyiv is holding on. So, at least that's positive news. We may only have enough food left for a couple of weeks, but Kyiv stands. Which means, we will, too.

MARIIA TSVIT
I don't know how our guys are able to do it. They're amazing.

ELEONORA
There are two things I don't understand. Why did I come here? And where is the father of my child?

KOLIA KHROMYI
The star has wept rose-color in the heart of your ears, the infinite rolled white from your nape to the small of your back, the sea has broken russet at your vermilion nipples, and Man bled black at your royal side.[24]

ARTEM *appears on the main screen with a yellow-blue background.*

ARTEM
I love you, my joy.

ELEONORA
(*laughing*)
> Finally, my love! I'm so happy to see and hear you!
> Be happy for me. I no longer use dirty words.

ARTEM
> I'm happy for you. And for our son, too. You need
> to live.

ELEONORA
> We'll see. It's all in God's hands! But you go,
> I beg you, because I may begin to cry. And
> I shouldn't do that. This Ukrainian guy in my
> belly wouldn't like that.

ARTEM
> It's a shame that it all turned out this way.

ELEONORA
> It's all in God's hands.

OLENA VOLODYMYRIVNA
> Yes, it's all in God's hands.

ELEONORA
> The only true help when things go badly is the
> Mother of God. You need to pray to her, and
> She'll take care of everything. I'm telling you,
> that's the way it is. A certain woman whom
> I used to know could not have children for a long
> time. She visited doctors so many times it's hard
> to count. She spent so much money on this. And
> then she was advised to travel to Nazareth, to the

Mother of God. And she did. She prayed there for a week. And she finally became pregnant. And now, a year later, her husband has perished. She's so pregnant, with such large breasts, and now she's alone. She sits here with you and laughs.

MARIIA TSVIT
I have such hopelessness and such helplessness in my heart. I want to go to Ukraine so much!

VASIA TSVIT
We are in Ukraine, Mariia.

MARIIA TSVIT
We are in occupied territories! There is no Ukraine here! People are already afraid to speak Ukrainian. Today, I heard how people who live in the neighboring co-op, who would always speak in Ukrainian because it is their native language, now speak Russian to one another. And it was so awful, so painful, so unbearable!

VASIA TSVIT
Listen to me. We are Ukraine. Do you understand? All of us are who we are. Including everyone who speaks Ukrainian and everyone who doesn't. And even those who tend to quickly adjust when needed. Everyone who is in despair and is hopeless. And everyone who hangs on and helps others to hang on. Blyzhni Sady is Ukraine. It's just that it's a small, isolated Ukraine. And, perhaps, one that's not needed by anyone. That's almost invisible. But without us, that other, big

Ukraine doesn't exist either. It doesn't exist, Mariia. A Ukraine that would not always think about us, that is not us, does not exist!

STEPAN HRYHOROVYCH
(*smiling sadly*)
I doubt anyone thinks about us. I doubt it. And if they do, then it's just two or three people. One's family and friends.

MARIIA TSVIT
Ah, who possibly needs us, Vasia...

VASIA TSVIT
I'll say it again. (*He rises and stands in front of everyone.*) Stepan Hryhorovych! Olena Volodymyrivna! Mar'iana! You and I, Eleonora, and even Ophelia. All of us together—we are Ukraine!

OPHELIA
I speak exclusively in Ukrainian. Look how well I know it. (*She rises and stands next to Vasia, in front of everyone.*)

Whether 'tis nobler in the mind to suffer
The slings and arrows of outrageous fortune,
Or to take arms against a sea of troubles,
And, by opposing, end them? To die, to sleep—
No more—and by a sleep to say we end
The heartache and the thousand natural shocks
That flesh is heir to—'tis a consummation
Devoutly to be wished. To die, to sleep.
To sleep, perchance to dream—ay, there's the rub...[25]

How do you like it?

Everyone applauds.

STEPAN HRYHOROVYCH
How beautifully the girl recites, how beautifully.
I, too, loved to recite in my youth but later went
into machine operations. The Terebovlia School
of Culture—that's my alma mater.

MAR'IANA
Wow. That's where I went to school as well.

*Kazymyr rises, stands to the left of Vasia, and not so
much speaks as recites.*

KAZYMYR
So that you know, the main goal of the
Terebovlia school is to train highly-qualified
specialists in various fields. The Terebovlia
Higher School of Culture is a higher educational
institute with level I–II accreditation in the
training of young specialists. All the conditions
for getting a professional education are there,
the instructors there are very qualified. This was
a brief commercial break. (*He bows.*)

Everyone applauds.

MAR'IANA
What major?

STEPAN HRYHOROVYCH
Spectacles and Theatrical Events. By the way,
my specialization is very honorable: Director of a
Drama Troupe.

VASIA TSVIT
Wow! How appropriate.

KAZYMYR
Yes, it really fits the situation.

VASIA TSVIT
What a pleasant surprise, Stepan Hryhorovych!

STEPAN HRYHOROVYCH
(*respectfully*)
The Terebovlia region, for your information, is
famous for its theatrical professional and amateur
arts. (*He turns to Ophelia.*) But excuse me, I always
wanted to ask you. Which co-op are you from,
young lady? I can't seem to remember you at all.

OLENA VOLODYMYRIVNA
(*to Stepan Hryhorovych*)
Lay off the girl.

OPHELIA
Hamlet, Prince of Denmark.

STEPAN HRYHOROVYCH
I see, I see. To be or not to be—that is the
question. Very fashionable. Must be by one of
the new writers.

DANYLO ANDRIIOVYCH
What dreams will we have after we die?

KAZYMYR
I would like to point out that, although I'm a crow, I'm Ukraine too.

STEPAN HRYHOROVYCH
That is correct, the birds of Ukraine are Ukraine, too.

VASIA TSVIT
I have no doubt that the Corvus that live in Ukraine are Ukraine! Or, let's say, Danylo Andriiovych, my grandfather. He died a long time ago, but so what? Many people have died. Every one of us could die. But, regardless of that, we remain Ukrainians! A part of us will remain. Through memory. Through faith and strength.

OLENA VOLODYMYRIVNA
(*to Danylo Andriiovych*)
Your grandson is wonderful, a beautiful and talented person!

DANYLO ANDRIIOVYCH
Thank you very much, Olena.

VASIA TSVIT
And Kolia Khromyi is Ukraine, too! Even if he's completely insane, right Kolia? (*He embraces Kolia*.) And his insanity is a national Ukrainian one, because it is the result of the meeting

between a Ukrainian and the damn Russians. Our traditional spiritual malady. Both our visible and invisible worlds are contained in it! To be a part of existence, of faith, and immortality. They have been murdering us for three hundred years, destroying our culture for three hundred years. And that is why, in Kolia's insanity, there are so many literary allusions and quotes. (*He laughs.*) But notice that they all have roots in the European cultural heritage, which cannot but delight us.

KAZYMYR

Corvus is a real bird with only a little bit of illusion. Just a bit.

MARIIA TSVIT

Fine, Vasia, we are Ukraine, fine. But we can't do anything. We can't rescue ourselves. We have nothing to ride in. We can't go on foot. There are constant explosions and Russians everywhere.

STEPAN HRYHOROVYCH

To cross the checkpoint by foot? How much time would that take? And they won't let you though anyway.

MARIIA TSVIT

So, what are the options then? Lie down and die? Vasia—ask Danylo Andriiovych or Kazymyr what we should do. Can this really be all there is? Does it come down to simply waiting for death?

VASIA TSVIT
  There is no Danylo Andriiovych. He died twenty
  years ago. Get a hold of yourself. And there is no
  Kazymyr either. I made him up.

KAZYMYR
  I don't agree with this, Vasia. And, if I were in
  your shoes, I wouldn't categorically insist on this
  so much.

VASIA TSVIT
(*quietly, to Kazymyr*)
  Keep quiet.

ELEONORA
  You know what, that's what I thought, too, at
  the start. But now I see Danylo Andriiovych, he's
  sitting right there, and Crow-Kazymyr next to
  me, and Ophelia... And our impending death.

*VLADYSLAVA FEDORIVNA comes running from the gate
to the place where our protagonists sit.*

VLADYSLAVA FEDORIVNA
  Who is the head of management here? Are any
  one of you part of the leadership?

STEPAN HRYHOROVYCH
  Well, I'm the head, and what of it?

VLADYSLAVA FEDORIVNA
  My name is Vladyslava Fedorivna, and I have
  come to rescue you. In short: it's urgent that you

hang some white flags on the fences and on the gate! I ran over here from the homestead. The Russians are coming, they'll be here in an hour. They want to inspect the cottage communities. Hang some white flags! They say, they'll shoot at any homes that don't have white flags.

STEPAN HRYHOROVYCH
(*in a restrained manner*)
We're not going to hang anything. Take a hike, missy.

VLADYSLAVA FEDORIVNA
(*confidently, insistingly*)
Hang them up, I say. Before it's too late. Their guns can make holes like this in walls. (*She demonstrates the size of the holes.*)

MAR'IANA
Run along, lady, may God be with you.

Vladyslava Fedorivna makes a crooked smile in disbelief but does not leave the stage.

OLENA VOLODYMYRIVNA
Right on, Stepan.

ELEONORA
Let them suck on their white flags.

OLENA VOLODYMYRIVNA
It's getting dark. Time to scatter. Here, they can shoot all of us at once. But, if we're in our homes, maybe someone will survive.

MARIIA TSVIT
(*getting up*)
 Let's go home, Vasia. We'll await our so-called
 brothers from the north there. I'm sick of
 waiting for them. Let them come. These are their
 five minutes of fame.

VASIA TSVIT
 Why don't we enjoy a bottle or two of wine?

MARIIA TSVIT
 I'm all for it, my love.

VLADYSLAVA FEDORIVNA
 Have you all lost your minds? Did you not hear
 what I said? The Russians who came to the
 homestead ordered me to tell everyone that they
 will not shoot at those cottage homes that have
 white flags hanging on them. If they don't see
 them, then they will shoot those houses up, for
 sure. Do you hear what I'm saying?

STEPAN HRYHOROVYCH
 What kind of bullshit is that? There's no logic to
 it, it doesn't make any sense.

DANYLO ANDRIIOVYCH
 Please! Russians and sense?

VASIA TSVIT
 I'm convinced they will shoot at the homes with
 white flags first. They'll go after them first.
 Because they're Russians.

ELEONORA

Mother of God, thank you for everything!
I was an intellectual, I was married, and I was
pregnant. And now it is time to be happy. We're
coming to you, Artem, we're coming to you, our
husband and father. Lord (*she makes the sign of
the cross*), thank you for everything! (*She turns
to everyone and bows.*) And you, too, esteemed
ladies and gentlemen, thank you for your
wonderful company. You are true Ukrainians
and fantastic people. We spent some quality
time together.

KOLIA KHROMYI

(*rises and runs to the gate, yelling joyfully*)
I'll spin and run: where's the ray? Where's the
ray? I'll die as an evening sacrifice. And the
carousel horses will trample the poor creature.
I'll die as an evening sacrifice! I'll die as an
evening sacrifice! I'll die as an evening sacrifice![26]

KAZYMYR

Sorry, Vasia, but this time that's how it is.

VASIA TSVIT

Don't worry. In no way are you at fault. Because
you are actually just me.

DANYLO ANDRIIOVYCH

But the director of drama theater is correct this
time around. White flags should only be hung in
cars that have the word "Children" written on
them.

KAZYMYR
That's a shame. You may end up having to die.

VASIA TSVIT
Perhaps.

VLADYSLAVA FEDORIVNA
You're all nuts! All of you!
(*She shakes her head in shock, walks away.*)

STEPAN HRYHOROVYCH
Let's all go together. Dusk is falling. It still gets
dark rather early. Besides, it seems that there
are military vehicles up past that turn. You see,
they've pulled up to our neighbors. Move faster.
It's better to die in your own home.

*Everybody gets up and, as a group, go up to the gates of
Blyzhni Sady.*

An explosion. Shooting. The lights dim.

SCENE THREE

The bedroom in the Tsvit house. The ticking of the clock and the noise made by the furnace can be heard. From regular explosions, the invisible dishware in the china cabinet occasionally rings. Across from the bed, there is a large, round table set for dining. On it are bottles of wine, large festive wine glasses, homemade cookies pierced with three Ukrainian flags, walnuts in a clay bowl, honey in a small vase, and very thinly sliced bread on a separate plate.

Sitting around the table are MARIIA TSVIT, VASIA TSVIT, BABA KARPA, KOLIA KHROMYI, and ELEONORA. Kolia Khromyi, in the breaks between his remarks, very quietly and almost continuously sings Ukrainian folk songs. During the entire scene, KAZYMYR sits in his sofa chair.

Nine lit flashlights are on the table, similar to the ones we saw at the Tsvits' in earlier scenes.

The table and the characters are also shown on the main screen. The camera slowly moves around, showing honey, wine, very thinly sliced bread, faces, eyes, smiles, and Kolia Khromyi's singing.

BABA KARPA

You see, Kolia and I didn't bring you the flashlights for nothing. It really is better with the flashlights. Right?

KOLIA KHROMYI

And later someone broke the fence picket, pear-like lanterns hang from the tree enchantingly. The world opened up for the poet in that fence hole— the vast, complex, and impenetrable world.[27]

VASIA TSVIT

We only have two that are solar powered, so our evenings are always very dark.

BABA KARPA

Kolia and I bought such flashlights at the start of COVID. Kolia really likes flashlights. He can't fall asleep without them. He turns on the flashlights when it's still light out and then lies down in bed. He doesn't like the darkness. And, when it is quiet, he begins to cry.

KOLIA KHROMYI

(*speaks very fast, swinging his body back and forth, waving his hands*)

And only where waves, tired, return, where sand chokes in the waves, fulfilling its dreams, it is clear that there are many loyalties as there are betrayals, and as much faith as disbelief. And everything burns up like forests and is preserved like church silver. Silence only strengthens voices. Darkness only emphasizes light.[28]

ELEONORA
(*takes a very thinly sliced piece of bread and spreads a bit of honey on it*)
> You have bread! (*She laughs.*) I haven't seen any for three weeks.

MARIIA TSVIT
> Please, do have some more! We've got lots of everything! We've got more! Right, Vasia?

VASIA TSVIT
> Please, everyone, have some! Baba Karpa, Koliusia! Don't be sad. Kolia, why are you just singing and not eating? Look: cookies, honey, walnuts! Do you like sweets?

BABA KARPA
> When he gets really scared of something, he sings and recalls poems.

ELEONORA
> I'm so grateful that you invited me to your place. I would be scared and very sad if I were at home alone.

VASIA TSVIT
(*picks up a bottle of wine and pours*)
> So, what do you say we drink while we still have the time? Mariia, Eleonora, would you like a bit, too?

ELEONORA
> I don't know if I should...

VASIA TSVIT
> You can have a little bit. It's a very good wine!
> I bought it for our wedding anniversary.

MARIIA TSVIT
(*smiling*)
> And the honey and walnuts, too, by the way.

BABA KARPA
> And when will it be exactly, your anniversary?

VASIA TSVIT
> It has passed already. Mariia and I became
> husband and wife on the 24th, just as the war
> began. Yep, it is what it is.

BABA KARPA
> That's some anniversary.

VASIA TSVIT
> Yep. Kolia, I'm begging you, stop singing, have
> some honey and walnuts. I know you like them.

*Explosions. Somewhere nearby, very loud machine gun
and automatic rifle rounds can suddenly be heard.*

MARIIA TSVIT
(*looks at her wine glass*)
> Is that shooting taking place in the neighboring
> co-op?

VASIA TSVIT
Yes. In Copernicus, perhaps. I wonder if they
hung white flags or not. Alright then. I propose
we drink to our country. Let it live on! Let it
flower! Let us be victorious! To Ukraine!

KOLIA KHROMYI
I share the blazing credo on your flags. Let me
fall, if I must. As long as you go on.[29]

EVERYONE
(*in various directions*)
To Ukraine! (*Everyone drinks.*)

KOLIA KHROMYI
(*speaking very fast*)
Ukraine is a Baroque country. Wandering
through it—a feast for the eyes. And that is why
the eye gets a temptation: to ruin everything.
And no matter how much I'd travel...[30]

BABA KARPA
(*interrupts Kolia, offers him a piece of bread spread
with honey*)
Stop it for a moment! Take a piece of bread,
eat it. Take it, I'm talking to you! Attaboy! And
here's some tea I made especially for you, take
it, too. Don't topple it over, I'm talking to you!
Kolia, you are a grown man. (*She wipes the tea
that Kolia does end up spilling with a napkin.*)

*Very loud machine gun and automatic rifle rounds are
heard.*

MARIIA TSVIT
Oh God, Vasia, that's from somewhere out on our street. It's so close now.

BABA KARPA
No, I think it's still coming from the neighboring co-op. It's from over there. It's past the fence. It's not here yet.

ELEONORA
But, for some reason, I'm not scared. All of this, nonetheless, will have to end. Don't you sense this as well?

MARIIA TSVIT
Sense what?

ELEONORA
Well, the sense that we all—that is, residents and Ukrainians of Blyzhni Sady, at least those that find themselves in this room now—ended a long time ago. That is, not that we have died, but that everything has been determined my someone already. Everything has been determined, all parts and roles have been assigned. We've pulled it off and have exhausted ourselves as people. Completely exhausted ourselves, with nothing left. And there is no need to fear! Just don't be afraid! There's no need!

VASIA TSVIT
I don't really understand what you are getting at. I don't feel like I've completely exhausted

myself. I don't think I've even realized who I've been. And why.

MARIIA TSVIT
Maybe you're right, Elia. We shouldn't be afraid. But it still is terrifying. My fingers are becoming numb, and something has been fluttering in my chest for forty minutes nonstop. And I can't do anything about it. (*She drinks what's left in her glass in large gulps.*)

BABA KARPA
And something is fluttering in my stomach, too. And I can tell you (*laughing*) that it's not butterflies. A serpent is fluttering, a serpent, black and cold.

KOLIA KHROMYI
Now I'm doomed forever! I've been abandoned by Aeneas, poor me, like the lowest scum, Aeneas—he is an evil serpent, not a man![31]

ELEONORA
(*turns to the audience*)
I get the feeling that we are all sitting on some kind of immeasurable stage at a round, meager table. On the table are honey, walnuts, cookies, wine and flashlights. Death is all around, somewhere people are screaming. They are being killed by the insane Russian culture which soon, in five, or maybe in ten minutes, or in half an hour, will arrive here. And will begin killing us, too. And that there is an audience in the hall.

They are sitting quietly and watching how you and me, my dear fellow co-op residents, are spending our final minutes. How we part with one another. How we part with our lives. And those people who are watching us from that hall that is filled to the brim, they are already there, in that time, where Victory has already arrived, where Ukraine is free. Where we are all forgiven and remembered, remembered and avenged. Avenged, remembered, and holy.

VASIA TSVIT
(*smiling in wonder*)
> Spot on. We are in a theater. Maybe even in Kyiv itself. Or, even better, in a rebuilt anew Mariupol, or in Kharkiv. Or maybe in Odesa, in Ivano-Frankivsk, or Chernivtsi.

BABA KARPA
> In Ukrainian Donetsk.

ELEONORA
> In Luhansk and Uzhhorod. In Lutsk, Kherson, and Mykolaiv. In Vinnytsia and Sumy.

MARIIA TSVIT
> In Lviv, that beautiful city of the lion.

VASIA TSVIT
(*gets up from the stool and the table with a wine glass in his hand*)
> In Crimea. My friends, we are in Crimea. The stage is located outside on Yalta's promenade. We hear

the crashing of waves, stars hang above us and twinkle. A lighthouse's traffic signals reach our stage where we drink wine and tea. The motor ships blow their horns, and seagulls screech.

The crashing of waves can be heard. The motor ship enters the port blowing its horn. The light from the Yalta lighthouse periodically flashes a band of light. Now and then, until the end of the scene, we hear the screeching of seagulls.

MARIIA TSVIT
Unbelievably large stars. Can you smell those almond trees?

BABA KARPA
Magnolia and lilac.

KOLIA KHROMYI
A girl's tender voice can be heard, a white seagull from blue shores.[32]

VASIA TSVIT
It's just theater. It just a kind of theater. Everything, it is true, ended long ago. Everything has passed. Nothing pains us. We are characters in a play about the very beginning of the war-torn spring of the year two thousand twenty-two. The director and writer of the play sit in the first row and are anxious, while we drink tea, hear gun shots, which are not heard in Yalta. The viewers of this play only hear the screeching of seagulls and the horns of motor ships.

MARIIA TSVIT
    And kids on the city beach.

Suddenly, a heavy knock is heard on the door of the Tsvit home. The screeching of seagulls becomes quieter. Everyone looks at one another. Vasia Tsvit places his wine glass on the table, pulls out a small axe from under it. He looks around at everyone and goes to the door. Some voices are heard and suddenly Vasia Tsvit reappears together with STEPAN HRYHOROVYCH, OLENA VOLODYMYRIVNA, and MAR'IANA.

VASIA TSVIT
(*joyfully*)
    What wonderful guests have arrived!

STEPAN HRYHOROVYCH
    Sorry if we're intruding, but sitting at home seemed silly to us. We decided to join you. (*He places a bottle of nalyvka on the table.*) We brought our homemade nalyvka.

OLENA VOLODYMYRIVNA
(*places a large plate on the table*)
    And a cake. It's delicious. It's my mom's recipe and I bake it all the time.

MAR'IANA
    I couldn't remain alone, either. Moreover, because Ostap, my brother, perished, somehow a text message from his friend got through to me. They killed my brother, killed him. (*She cries*

quietly.) And I can't even call anyone there to find out how and why...

MARIIA TSVIT
My God, Mar'iana! (*She hugs her, tries to cheer her up.*) Have a seat, please, have a seat.

VASIA TSVIT
Please, please. Sit down!

As soon as everyone sits down, a horrible explosion is heard. The women scream. The sounds of automatic gun rounds being shot are heard. Another explosion. The room becomes completely filled with darkness. Silence.

After a minute, a light comes on. And it is not the Chinese solar-charged flashlights but a large chandelier above the table. The room looks different. The furniture is different. There are mirrors on the walls. The sea and mountains are visible in the window. More people have gathered at the table. Present are: ARTEM, OSTAP, KOSTIANTYN, HRYHORII, LIUBOV PAVLIVNA and PAVLYK, SERAPHYMA and SERAPHYMA'S HUSBAND, SERHII, and INNA on whose lap the DOG from the first act sits and eats something from her palm.

Gradually, the screeching of seagulls and horns of the motor ships return. The crashing of waves becomes very pronounced and loud.

On the main screen, a map of Ukraine, composed of countless conversation windows, is turned on.

VASIA TSVIT

My dear ones, we are finally on the stage. And
where else should we be. (*He smiles.*) On a big
Ukrainian stage. And we are never alone on this
stage. Because we are all together. The young
and the old. The perished and the living. Those
who wished for Victory and those who achieved
it. Those who lost faith and fell. Those who rose
and kept going. Faith and dignity are with us.

ELEONORA

And genuine hatred, Vasia, genuine hatred.

MARIIA TSVIT

And love, Vasia, and love.

MAR'IANA

And has life ended?

BABA KARPA

Don't spew nonsense. It's all still ahead of us.

VASIA TSVIT

Fill your glasses, friends! Don't just sit there, fill
'em up! This is a celebration of immortality! A
celebration of the theater of life, I'm telling you!
An otherworldly celebration! Fill your glasses
and drink!

SERAPHYMA

(*to the audience, in a close-up on the main screen*)

Those who have not yet reached Victory—know
that it is coming!

LIUBOV PAVLIVNA
(*to the audience, in a close-up on the main screen*)
   Those who continue to live after Victory—
   remember that we existed!

KOLIA KHROMYI
   Can Hamlet finally get some wine?

The characters pour drinks, laugh, talk among themselves.
The screeching of seagulls and horns of the motor ships
resume.

An explosion. The lights dim.

The End

Ternopil
June-July 2022

NOTES

1 From the popular Ukrainian song "Stoït' hora vysokaia" (There is a high mountain). Text by Leonid Hlibov (1827–1893), music by Mykola Lysenko (1818–1897) (tr.).

2 In Ukraine, a *nalyvka* is usually a homemade liqueur—a sweet alcoholic beverage containing 15–35% of alcohol by volume (with or without added rectified sprit), often made with fruits or berries from one's own orchard or a forest nearby (tr., ed.).

3 These lines are from "Svit nadzvychaino shyrokyi..." (The world is remarkably wide, 1957) by Lina Kostenko (tr.).

4 In the original, these lines are from Lina Kostenko's poem "Ia vyrosla u Kyïvs´kii Venetsiï..." (I grew up in Kyivan Venice, 1980). The first stanza, recited by Kolia, describes a flood at Trukhaniv Island near Kyiv and is rendered in the most basic rhyme scheme (AAAA), producing a couplet-like, children's song effect. Kolia's recitation appears to be part of his PTSD from torture, triggered by sound alone (in Ukrainian, informatsiia in Stepan Hryhorovych's question rhymes with Venetsiia, akatsiia, inertsiia, and komunikatsiia in the stanza) (tr., ed.).

5 Izoliatsiia (Isolation) is a former insulation materials factory and, since the takeover by the Russia-sponsored militia and Russian special forces, an illegal prison in Donetsk that has gained notoriety for the widespread use of torture. An account of incarceration in Izoliatsiia can be found in Stanislav Aseyev's, *The Torture Camp on Paradise Street* (Cambridge, Mass.: Harvard Ukrainian Research Institute, 2023) (ed.).

6 From Hamlet, Act 5, Scene 1, by William Shakespeare (tr.).

7   From Hamlet, Act 1, Scene 1, by William Shakespeare (tr.).
8   These lines are from the poetic drama *Oderzhyma* (A woman possessed, 1901) by Lesia Ukrainka (Larysa Kosach) (tr.).
9   See note 1 above (tr.).
10 These lines are from the poem "Zakhodyt' chorne sontse dnia..." (The day's black sun sets, 1976) by Vasyl' Stus (tr.).
11 These lines are also from the poem "Zakhodyt' chorne sontse dnia..." (The day's black sun sets, 1976) by Vasyl' Stus (tr.).
12 These lines are from the poem "Tovaryshtsi na spomyn" (To my friend, as a recollection, 1896) by Lesia Ukrainka (Larysa Kosach) (tr.).
13 From Hamlet, Act 4, Scene 5, by William Shakespeare (tr.).
14 This is a line from the poem "Synia dalechin'" (The blue distance, 1920) by Maksym Ryl's'kyi (tr.).
15 From Hamlet, Act 4, Scene 5, by William Shakespeare (tr.).
16 Again from Hamlet, Act 4, Scene 5, by William Shakespeare (tr.).
17 A reference to the poem "Zapovit" (The testament, 1845) by Taras Shevchenko (tr.).
18 In Slavic folklore, "living water" (*zhyva voda*) brings the dead back to life (tr.).
19 These lines are from the poem "Zhertva vechirnia" (The evening sacrifice, 1919) by Mykhail' Semenko (tr.).
20 Here, the author is quoting lines from Pavlo Tychyna's Ukrainian-language translation of Rainer Maria Rilke's poem "Die Stille" (Silence, 1902) from the latter's *Das Buch der Bilder* (The book of images). The English-language translation of "Die Stille" used in this volume is by Edward Snow and is found in Rainer Maria Rilke, *The Book of Images: A Bilingual Edition*, trans. by Edward Snow (San Francisco: North Point Press, 1991), 27.
21 Another quote from Pavlo Tychyna's Ukrainian-language translation of Rainer Maria Rilke's poem "Die Stille" (Silence, 1902) from the latter's *Das Buch der Bilder* (The book of images). The English-language translation here is again by Edward Snow from *The Book of Images*, 27.

22 This reference is steeped in symbolism: during the coup d'etat that ushered in the collapse of the Soviet Union, the Soviet state-owned TV channels broadcasted Tchaikovsky's *Swan Lake* instead of news or other programming. Since then, this ballet on television has come to represent hope for the fall of Vladimir Putin's repressive regime (ed.).

23 These lines are from the poem "Zhertva vechirnia" (The evening sacrifice, 1919) by Mykhail' Semenko (tr.).

24 These lines are from the poem "L'étoile a pleuré rose" (The star wept pink, 1871) by Artur Rimbaud. The English-language translation here is by Olivier Bernard, originally published in 1962 in Artur Rimbaud, *Collected Poems*, quoted here from *Artur Rimbaud*, https://www.mag4.net/Rimbaud/poesies/Star.html (tr.).

25 In the original, a Ukrainian translation of Hamlet's monologue from Hamlet, Act 3, Scene 1, by William Shakespeare (tr.).

26 These lines are from the poem "Zhertva vechirnia" (The evening sacrifice, 1919) by Mykhail' Semenko (tr.).

27 These lines are from the poem "Slaidy" (Slides, 1980) by Lina Kostenko (tr.).

28 These lines are from the poem "Todi pochynaiet'sia vechir, same todi…" (When evening begins, exactly then, 2016) by Serhiy Zhadan (tr.).

29 These lines are from the poem "Ty synim nebom dyvyshsia na mene…" (You look at me through a blue sky, 1964) by Hryhorii Chubai (tr.).

30 These lines are from poem no. 10 by Yuri Andrukhovych in his cycle of poems *Lysty v Ukraïnu* (Letters to Ukraine, 1990) (tr.).

31 These lines are from Part One of Ivan Kotliarevskyi's *Eneïda* (The Aeneid, 1798), in which Dido laments the fact that Aeneas has left her (tr.).

32 These lines are from the poem "Divochyi holos dolita laskavyi…" (A girl's tender voice can be heard, 1958) by Maksym Ryl's'kyi (tr.).

Harvard Library of Ukrainian Literature
Recently Published

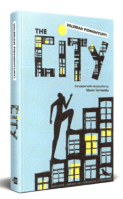

The City: A Novel
Valerian Pidmohylnyi

Translated with an introduction by Maxim Tarnawsky

This novel was a landmark event in the history of Ukrainian literature. Written by a master craftsman in full control of the texture, rhythm, and tone of the text, the novel tells the story of Stepan, a young man from the provinces who moves to the capital of Ukraine, Kyiv, and achieves success as a writer through a succession of romantic encounters with women.

2025	491 pp.	
ISBN 9780674291119 (cloth)		$39.95
9780674291126 (paperback)		$19.95
9780674291133 (epub)		
9780674291140 (PDF)		

Harvard Library of Ukrainian Literature, vol. 13

Read the book online

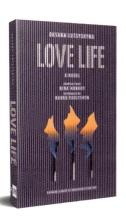

Love Life: A Novel
Oksana Lutsyshyna

Translated by Nina Murray | Introduced by Marko Pavlyshyn

The second novel of the award-winning Ukrainian writer and poet Oksana Lutsyshyna writes the story of Yora, an immigrant to the United States from Ukraine. A delicate soul that's finely attuned to the nuances of human relations, Yora becomes enmeshed in a relationship with Sebastian, a seductive acquaintance who seems to be suggesting that they share a deep bond. After a period of despair and complex grief that follows the end of the relationship, Yora is able to emerge stronger, in part thanks to the support from a friendly neighbor who has adapted well to life on the margins of society.

2024	276 pp.	
ISBN 9780674297159 (cloth)		$39.95
9780674297166 (paperback)		$19.95
9780674297173 (epub)		
9780674297180 (PDF)		

Harvard Library of Ukrainian Literature, vol. 12

Read the book online

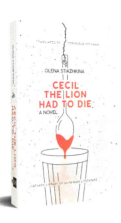

Cecil the Lion Had to Die:
A Novel

Olena Stiazhkina

Translated by Dominique Hoffman

This novel follows the fate of four families as the world around them undergoes radical transformations when the Soviet Union unexpectedly implodes, independent Ukraine emerges, and neoimperial Russia begins its war by occupying Ukraine's Crimea and parts of the Donbas. A tour de force of stylistic registers and intertwining stories, ironic voices and sincere discoveries, this novel is a must-read for those who seek to deeper understand Ukrainians from the Donbas, and how history and local identity have shaped the current war with Russia.

2024	248 pp.	
ISBN 9780674291645 (cloth)		$39.95
9780674291669 (paperback)		$19.95
9780674291676 (epub)		
9780674291683 (PDF)		

Harvard Library of Ukrainian Literature, vol. 11

Read
the book
online

Earth Gods:
Writings from before the War

Taras Prokhasko

Translated by Ali Kinsella, Mark Andryczyk and Uilleam Blacker
Introduced by Mark Andryczyk

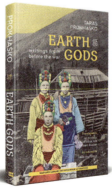

This book presents Taras Prokhasko's early writings: genre-bending *Anna's Other Days*, the collection of reflections *FM Galicia*, and *The UnSimple*, an iconoclastic novel that offers an alternative history of the Ukrainian Carpathian mountains of the first half of the twentieth century. Collected here for the first time in one volume, these stylistically and conceptually virtuosic texts testify to the richness of contemporary Ukrainian literature.

2025	appr. 400 pp.	
ISBN 9780674291164 (hardcover)		$39.95
9780674291171 (paperback)		$19.95
9780674291188 (epub)		
9780674291195 (PDF)		

Harvard Library of Ukrainian Literature, vol. 10

Read
the book
online

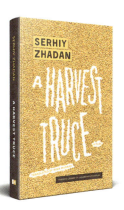

A Harvest Truce: A Play

Serhiy Zhadan

Translated by Nina Murray

Brothers Anton and Tolik reunite at their family home to bury their recently deceased mother. An otherwise natural ritual unfolds under extraordinary circumstances: their house is on the front line of a war ignited by Russian-backed separatists in eastern Ukraine.

Spring 2023

ISBN 9780674291997 (hardcover) — $29.95
9780674292017 (paperback) — $19.95
9780674292024 (epub)
9780674292031 (PDF)

Harvard Library of Ukrainian Literature, vol. 9

Read the book online

Cassandra: A Dramatic Poem

Lesia Ukrainka (Larysa Kosach)

Translated by Nina Murray, introduction by Marko Pavlyshyn

The classic myth of Cassandra turns into much more in Lesia Ukrainka's rendering: Cassandra's prophecies are uttered in highly poetic language—fitting to the genre of the dramatic poem that Ukrainka crafts for this work—and are not believed for that very reason, rather than because of Apollo's curse. Cassandra's being a poet and a woman are therefore the two focal points of the drama.

2024 | 263 pp, bilingual ed. (Ukrainian, English)

ISBN 9780674291775 (hardcover) — $29.95
9780674291782 (paperback) — $19.95
9780674291799 (epub)
9780674291805 (PDF)

Harvard Library of Ukrainian Literature, vol. 8

Read the book online

Ukraine, War, Love: A Donetsk Diary

Olena Stiazhkina

Translated by Anne O. Fisher

In this war-time diary, Olena Stiazhkina depicts day-to-day developments in and around her beloved hometown during Russia's 2014 invasion and occupation of the Ukrainian city of Donetsk.

Summer 2023

ISBN 9780674291690 (hardcover)	$39.95
9780674291706 (paperback)	$19.95
9780674291713 (epub)	
9780674291768 (PDF)	

Harvard Library of Ukrainian Literature, vol. 7

Read the book online

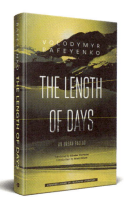

The Length of Days: An Urban Ballad

Volodymyr Rafeyenko

Translated by Sibelan Forrester
Afterword and interview with the author by Marci Shore

This novel is set mostly in the composite Donbas city of Z—an uncanny foretelling of what this letter has come to symbolize since February 24, 2022, when Russia launched a full-scale invasion of Ukraine. Several embedded narratives attributed to an alcoholic chemist-turned-massage therapist give insight into the funny, ironic, or tragic lives of people who remained in the occupied Donbas after Russia's initial aggression in 2014.

2023 | 349 pp.

ISBN 780674291201 (cloth)	$39.95
9780674291218 (paper)	$19.95
9780674291225 (epub)	
9780674291232 (PDF)	

Harvard Library of Ukrainian Literature, vol. 6

Read the book online

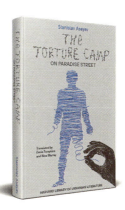

The Torture Camp on Paradise Street

Stanislav Aseyev

Translated by Zenia Tompkins and Nina Murray

Ukrainian journalist and writer Stanislav Aseyev details his experience as a prisoner from 2015 to 2017 in a modern-day concentration camp overseen by the Federal Security Bureau of the Russian Federation (FSB) in the Russian-controlled city of Donetsk. This memoir recounts an endless ordeal of psychological and physical abuse, including torture and rape, inflicted upon the author and his fellow inmates over the course of nearly three years of illegal incarceration spent largely in the prison called Izoliatsiia (Isolation).

2023	300 pp., 1 map, 18 ill.
ISBN 9780674291072 (cloth)	$39.95
9780674291089 (paper)	$19.95
9780674291102 (epub)	
9780674291096 (PDF)	

Harvard Library of Ukrainian Literature, vol. 5

Read the book online

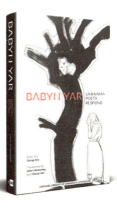

Babyn Yar: Ukrainian Poets Respond

Edited with introduction by Ostap Kin

Translated by John Hennessy and Ostap Kin

In 2021, the world commemorated the 80th anniversary of the massacres of Jews at Babyn Yar. The present collection brings together for the first time the responses to the tragic events of September 1941 by Ukrainian Jewish and non-Jewish poets of the Soviet and post-Soviet periods, presented here in the original and in English translation by Ostap Kin and John Hennessy.

2022	282 pp.
ISBN 9780674275591 (hardcover)	$39.95
9780674271692 (paperback)	$16.00
9780674271722 (epub)	
9780674271739 (PDF)	

Harvard Library of Ukrainian Literature, vol. 4

Read the book online

The Voices
of Babyn Yar

Marianna Kiyanovska

Translated by Oksana Maksymchuk and Max Rosochinsky
Introduced by Polina Barskova

With this collection of stirring poems, the award-winning Ukrainian poet honors the victims of the Holocaust by writing their stories of horror, death, and survival in their own imagined voices.

2022	192 pp.	
ISBN 9780674268760 (hardcover)		$39.95
9780674268869 (paperback)		$16.00
9780674268876 (epub)		
9780674268883 (PDF)		

Harvard Library of Ukrainian Literature, vol. 3

Read
the book
online

Mondegreen: Songs about
Death and Love

Volodymyr Rafeyenko

Translated and introduced by Mark Andryczyk

Volodymyr Rafeyenko's novel explores the ways that memory and language construct our identity, and how we hold on to it no matter what. The novel tells the story of Haba Habinsky, a refugee from Ukraine's Donbas region, who has escaped to the capital city of Kyiv at the onset of the Ukrainian-Russian war.

2022	204 pp.	
ISBN 9780674275577 (hardcover)		$39.95
9780674271708 (paperback)		$19.95
9780674271746 (epub)		
9780674271760 (PDF)		

Harvard Library of Ukrainian Literature, vol. 2

Read
the book
online